INVISIBLE EYELASHES

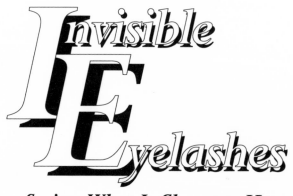

Invisible Eyelashes

Seeing What Is Closest to Us

by Nikkyo Niwano

translated by
James M. Vardaman

Kosei Publishing Co. • Tokyo

This book was originally published in Japanese under the title *Mienai Matsuge: Shiawase ni Naru Mono no Mikata.*

Editing by Joy S. Sobeck and Gary Hoiby. Cover design by Nobu.

First English edition, 1994

ISBN 4-333-01681-9   LCC Card No. applied for

CONTENTS

BE TRUE TO YOURSELF

THE TWO FUNCTIONS OF A CELL

THE WIND BLOWING
FROM THE FUTURE

EDITORIAL NOTE

In this book the names of all premodern Japanese are given in the Japanese style, with the surname first, and those of all modern (post-1868) Japanese are given in the Western style, with the surname last.

PROLOGUE

Many people refuse to believe in anything that cannot be proved logically or scientifically. Buddhists believe, however, that there is an orderly logic at work in the world. Since the ordinary eye cannot see this order, Buddhists try to see it with the eye of faith. In today's secular world, faith sometimes seems like an outdated or unnecessary concept. But if we look closely, we can see it operating every day in our lives. Here is an example, from Japan, of the kind of faith we employ in our relations with loved ones:

In the mountains of Shinshu a small group of students from Tokyo was gathering plant specimens, and just below the edge of a sheer cliff they found an unusual flower. They wanted to add it to their collection, but could not climb down far enough. They decided to tie pieces of clothing into a rope, down which one of them could climb. The rope seemed too flimsy, however, to support an adult. Just then a thirteen-year-old boy happened by. They asked him if he would be willing to climb down to the flower for a small reward while they stood above and held the rope. The boy refused. They doubled their offer, but he shook his head. They tripled and even quadrupled it, but still he refused. Finally they asked how much he wanted. The boy said, "I'll do it if my father holds the rope." This was faith. Logically, the boy would have been safer with several husky students holding the rope than with just his father. His trust in his father was not strictly logical.

The Japanese poet Jukichi Yagi (1898–1927), who died young, was a devout Christian. One of his poems expresses his faith succinctly:

> Because one calls,
> Something appears.
> Because one does not call,
> Something disappears.

When we call the name of God, certainly we feel something. Even if we cannot see God, we can feel the embrace of God. The same thing is true when we call the Buddha's name.

The poet Yaichi Aizu (1881–1956), who was born in Niigata Prefecture and became a professor emeritus of Waseda University, included the following poem in his *Jichu Rokumei-shu* (An Annotated Collection of Deer Cries):

> Eye of the Buddha old and faded
> On the temple wall watching over me.

Aizu was looking at a mural at the temple Horyu-ji in Nara Prefecture. No doubt as he opened his heart to the image of the Buddha, whose color had faded with time, he began to feel palpably that the Buddha was watching over him. Though the gods and buddhas may not be visible to the eye, those who believe in them can continually commune with them in spirit.

Buddhism teaches that when all living beings are purified, the world will be pure. A nation whose people enjoy peace and prosperity is not something that we should passively await. It is when its people become of one heart that a nation becomes serene and peaceful; when they are not of one heart, the nation is racked by contention and covetousness.

For this to take place, it is vital that each of us should grow spiritually. One cannot command others to do this, as one might order people to stand in line. Rather, each person must cleanse their own heart and behavior. Where can we undergo this spiritual training? In our own workplaces and our own homes.

The Japanese word for training hall, *dojo,* brings to mind a place where people practice judo or *kendo* (Japanese swordsmanship). Actually, the original meaning of *dojo* is the place where the Buddha attained enlightenment. He attained enlightenment at Bodh Gaya, preached for the first time at Sarnath, and after devoting the remaining fifty years of his life imparting his truths, died peacefully at Kushinagara. But the Lotus Sutra, one of Mahayana Buddhism's key scriptures, teaches that *wherever we are* is the training hall where the Buddha attained enlightenment, where he preached his first sermon, and where he entered nirvana.

In other words, it is in our everyday lives, as we diligently go about our work, that we should awaken to our true selves, focus our efforts on being considerate of those around us, and build a world filled with tranquillity. Each day, each bit of work, each encounter with someone—these are what is important. Despite this, do we not spend our days becoming angry, being avaricious, quarreling, and talking about our values without putting them into practice?

The reason we live like this is that each of us often seeks happiness for just ourselves. We think simplistically and compete with those around us, believing that unless we defeat them we will be unable to achieve our own happiness.

We often seem to be waiting for leaders to appear and teach us how to create a better world. But one who is respected as a leader is not necessarily one who is trying to teach something. People follow someone who earnestly seeks the right path and devotedly follows it. Each of us must become the kind of person who shows others the way, and it is a world of such people that we must create.

To manifest our true merit, it is important that we begin by fixing our gaze on whatever is nearest at hand. We cannot see what is really closest to us—our eyelashes. Likewise, in daily life, we often overlook important matters which seem routine and familiar, but which nevertheless touch us deeply. This book will attempt to show why and how each of us should stop and think about what is the most important thing closest to us. By learning to understand such things in a fresh and profound way, each of us can find and follow the path to a peaceful and happier world.

ATTITUDE MAKES
ALL THE DIFFERENCE

Joy and Discontent

Everyone on earth wishes to be happy, but many people never do become truly content. From my own perspective, it seems that the reason they are not happy is that they do not try to feel the joy that exists in their immediate circumstances. There is actually no condition that can be called "happiness"; rather, there is only a *sense of being happy*.

For example, one person may think that a rainy day is gloomy while another may welcome the rain. The reality of the rain is one and the same, but the ways the two feel about it are exactly the opposite. The one who can rejoice in the rain is the one who is happier. The same is true of work. When trouble arises at work, there are some who want to give up in despair, and then there are others who see difficulties as a challenge and rouse themselves to action. It seems that happiness depends on how one looks at things, how one appraises things, and how one responds to things.

The root of the Japanese word for happiness, *shiawase*, matches this way of thinking perfectly. According to a major Japanese dictionary, *shiawase* is the noun form of a verb meaning "to act flexibly according to circumstances." The peace of mind one gains from such action is what we call happiness.

One of the teachings of Buddhism is that the whole universe is contained in a single thought of one individual (*ichinen sanzen*, or "three thousand realms in one mind"). It means that the world around us changes when we change our attitude.

To those who are discontented and irritable, all they see and hear is depressing. The world around them is like the unpleasant odor that surrounds a drainage ditch. In contrast, when we have a single thought that is bright and pure, everything around us is proportionately brighter and purer. When the weather improves, just look at how the blue sky spreads wider and wider and the banks of clouds dissipate as they are blown before the rising air currents. One must call forth this sort of updraft from within one's own heart.

Along with many people in the world who seem unable to feel happy, there are some who seem to be masters of the art of enjoying life. One was Tachibana Akemi (1812–68), a poet and scholar of Japanese classical literature. In *Dokurakugin* (Reciting Poetry for My Own Pleasure), a collection of fifty-two poems, he writes:

Pleasure is getting up in the morning
And seeing a blossom that had not been there
The day before.

Pleasure is awakening after a nap to find
Rain sprinkling the garden.

He expresses pleasure at such small things as the blossoming of a plant and a midday shower. One who has this eye for the joys of life can be said to be happy.

Tachibana lauds other pleasures:

Pleasure is filling the empty rice bin
Knowing there is enough for another month.

Pleasure is when a rare fish delicacy is served
And all the children relish it, exclaiming,
"That's good!"

Tachibana was a man who aimed at honest poverty. In his poems he straightforwardly expresses the joy of being able, because he has even a small income, to fill the rice bin when the bottom had been exposed, and of being able to have something good to eat for the first time in a long while. Herein lies the wisdom of being satisfied with little and experiencing great joy.

As happiness is not just an abstract notion, neither is misery. However, if one gets into the habit of being discontented and dissatisfied, then a feeling of displeasure will fasten on whatever takes place around one.

It appears that there are many people who feel

happiness only when they experience some great joy once or twice a year. But if instead of hoping for rare moments of great elation, they managed to find pleasure in small, everyday things, their lives would be much happier.

Even in our daily work, it is possible to see things through eyes of joy as Tachibana did:

Pleasure is talking with a co-worker at the next
   desk
About one's good work.

Pleasure is the animation that takes over
When urgent business suddenly comes in.

Pleasure is being thanked by a regular customer
And saying, "Thank *you*," exchanging smiles.

At work, though tough problems may come one right after another, we should not think of them as hardships, but as pleasures. We can encourage ourselves by believing that dealing with difficult tasks makes us stronger. With this attitude, work becomes fun.

In the late eighteenth century there lived in the village of Bizen, in what is now Okayama Prefecture, a man named Aburaya Yoichibe, who was in the habit of saying "Thank goodness" quite often. When he awoke in the morning and saw his mother's face, he would say, "Thank goodness," and when he saw his wife he would say the same thing. Villagers nicknamed him Grateful Yoichibe. Once he stumbled on a stone and injured his knee, and although blood poured from the wound, he said as always, "Thank goodness!" A villager who was with him asked him why he was so grateful even though he had been injured. He replied, "I'm thankful I got off with only a small scratch." Like Tachibana, Yoichibe knew the key to happiness.

There are many ups and downs in life. Some things seem fortunate and others not. If one is rebuked for a mistake at work, one can take comfort in accepting the rebuke as good medicine and vow to be more careful. Just as it used to be said in Japan that the world is as kind as it is cruel, if there is someone who reprimands, there is also someone who consoles. What is important is to see that the one who scolds is also a benefactor. Many executives of leading corporations say, "Now that I look back on it, the chagrin I felt at being reprimanded on a certain occasion became a great asset."

If one imitates the lifestyle of Tachibana or Grateful Yoichibe, one's world will be broadened and one will feel much more at ease. We should always keep in mind that whether we are happy or miserable is determined by how we see and respond to things.

A happy life begins with small pleasures, which greatly multiply.

Rose or Thorns?

The U.S. dollar went from ¥240 to almost ¥120 in 1986–87, and Japan's economic strength became recognized around the world. Though hardly an excuse for extravagance, the price of imports dropped by essentially half in two years. Despite all this, great discomfort was voiced in Japan concerning what such a strong yen would mean for the future.

The rose is beautiful, but its stem has many thorns—this is a fact. One person will say the rose is beautiful, but that it has thorns, stressing the negative. Another person will concede that there are thorns, but will insist on the rose's beauty, emphasizing the positive. When the matter at hand is the ability or other qualities of a human being, the ways in which one accepts someone can be just as various. If one comments, "He does good work and he's a pleasant fellow," and leaves it at that, everyone will be left in congenial spirits. Yet in every society there are faultfinders, who are not content unless they have noted some imperfection and can say something like, "He does good work, but he's overconfident and likes to boast." By dragging others down, such people hope to maintain a sense of superiority. If they could somehow apply the brakes before making critical comments, it would open up an entirely new world.

Near the gate of the temple Nanzen-ji in Kyoto, there once lived an old woman whom everyone called Tearful Granny. Rain or shine, she was always in tears. One day the chief priest asked her, "What could be so sad that it makes you cry all the time?" The old woman replied, "I have two sons, one an umbrella-maker at Sanjo and the other a sandal-maker at Gojo. When it rains, I know people won't want to go out and buy sandals from my first son, and that makes me sad. When the sun comes out, I realize people won't buy umbrellas from my second son, and I grieve over that." The priest said, "How about looking at it the other way around? When it rains, be glad that people will buy lots of umbrellas. When the weather improves, rejoice that your other son's sandal business will prosper." The old woman took his point. "You're right," she said, and from that day on she always smiled and lived happily.

Most people, when they hear this story, laugh at the old woman's foolishness. However, it is not something that can be so easily laughed away, because many people, big or small, think like this. By searching for the seeds of discontent in one's surroundings, one makes oneself unhappy.

Several people are climbing a mountain and become thirsty. There is not much water in the canteen, and when they divide it up, each person gets half a cup. "Why, I only get half a cup," grumbles one. "I'm glad I have at least half a cup to quench my thirst," says another, happily drinking it. It goes without saying which of the two is happier and the kind of person whom others find an agreeable companion.

Life is an accumulation of small happenings. This is precisely why the spiritual habit of looking at a rose and meekly accepting its beauty is of such great importance. Doing this is certainly not very difficult. All that is required is a momentary change of heart. Tearful Granny was able to reorient herself as a result of the priest's simple comment. Blessed today with an abundance of knowledge, we ought to be able to make such a conversion with our own strength through so-called self-awareness.

It goes without saying that this kind of spiritual practice is for our own happiness, but it also manifests great power when we meet and lead other people. If we look at others with a critical eye, our attitude turns caustic and we tend to heap spiteful remarks on them. Others only recoil from one who does this. On the other hand, if we look for others' strong points, we naturally meet them with "smiling faces and loving words"—one of the Buddha's "seven offerings that cost nothing." Our facial expressions become friendlier and we speak considerately. When we treat others this way, they naturally open their hearts. Furthermore, if others recognize their own strong points, they will gain confidence and courage.

It is important, when you are scolding someone, to recognize their merits. You might say something like, "You are always so careful; how come you made such a mistake?" Or, "This isn't very good, but recently you've been quite attentive to things." Recognition of the person's good points leaves a deeper impression than a scolding, giving the person greater confidence.

The adventurous skier Yuichiro Miura (b. 1932) took on challenges that defy common sense, such as skiing down the steep slope of Mount Fuji and down the South Col of Mount Everest from an altitude of 8,000 meters. He is said to have been sickly as a child. When he took the physical strength test for entry into high school, it was discovered that he had a heart defect. This discovery, along with frequent absences from elementary school due to illness, led to his failing the examination. Miura was completely disheartened and again took sick. His mother came to him and said, "In the future you're going to be a great person, so for right now it's all right for things to be this way." He took these words to heart and they provided the driving force that made him famous. No one knows what it was in Miura that his mother perceived. Somehow she sensed his special ability and had faith in it.

When you see a rose, accept its beauty with good grace. Generously acknowledge others' good points. If you do so, the circle of happiness that grows around you will spread to encompass others.

Those who only see a rose's thorns throw away the strength to live happily.

The Contents of Hotei's Sack

The more life offers, the more we want, until there is no end to our desires. We should not only use things to make life more pleasant, but respect the life of each thing we use and be grateful for all things. Unless we cultivate this feeling of gratitude, someday the world will surely be destroyed.

Hotei is one of Japan's seven deities of good fortune. His plump, smiling face is perfect for a deity of fortune and prosperity. Hotei is the Japanese name for Pu-tai, thought to have been a Chinese Chan priest of the Later Liang dynasty, revered as an incarnation of the Bodhisattva Maitreya. Hotei always has a large sack close at hand. Since he is a deity of good fortune, most people assume he is a kind of Santa Claus with a bag full of valuable things to divide among us. Nothing could be further from the truth. I am told that the sack is full of carefully sorted leftovers. Hotei is not a deity who brings good fortune, but rather a Chan priest who taught the virtue of frugality.

There is a deep significance in that. If one desires good fortune, one should waste nothing. This is the way of life Buddhism has traditionally taught since the Buddha's time—that wisdom is being satisfied with little.

The Buddha was first moved to seek the Way by his realization that no one escapes the sufferings of old age, sickness, and death. Yet even earlier, we are told, he had a formative experience when he saw small birds prey on insects that had been turned up by a plow. He thought deeply about why living things eat each other, and in the course of his spiritual training and discipline, he attained a much broader view of this issue. This view is evident in the first of Buddhism's five basic precepts for lay people, which is not to take life. Above all, this means not taking human life, but in a wider sense it means not taking any form of life thoughtlessly. The wasteful use of things is also a way of destroying life. All things, including the food we eat and the tools we use, have a life of their own. When full use is made of a life and it completely manifests its value, it has, in the Mahayana sense of the phrase, "attained buddha-hood." Throwing away things like leftovers without making full use of them is therefore a way of destroying life.

Since the Industrial Revolution, we have used machines and energy sources like petroleum and coal to manufacture goods in large quantities, and without our being fully aware of it, mass production has come to spur mass consumption. As a result, we have lost the spirit of taking care of things and have become irresponsible in how we use them. This sin of taking life thoughtlessly will always rebound against us.

What is now sharply pressing the advanced nations to reconsider their behavior is the law of entropy, which is one of the two laws of thermodynamics. Einstein asserted that this was the first law of all science. In simple terms it means that matter and energy move only in one direction—that is, they are transformed from the usable to the unusable. In other words, as we use the raw materials and energy sources of our planet, their quantities decrease. The only things that increase are waste products.

By using precious resources and energy, advanced countries try to make products that are useful. But if one looks just below the surface, one can see that what we are really doing is converting what is usable into something unusable. If the current situation continues, the planet's resources and energy will be exhausted, and humanity will eventually be ruined.

Prof. Jeremy Rifkin addresses this problem in his book *Entropy: A New World View:*

> Adherents of Eastern religions—and especially the Buddhists—have long understood the value of minimizing energy flow-through. . . . The Eastern religions have long claimed that unnecessary dissipation of personal energy only adds to the confusion and disorder of the world. Ultimate truth, according to Eastern doctrine, is arrived at only by becoming one with the world around you. This can only be accomplished by entering into a unified relationship with the rest of nature.

Professor Rifkin says that in Japan, one of the world's most highly industrialized nations, Buddhism and Confucianism are the most influential philosophies. Japan therefore respects the law of entropy. He says that in the course of its remarkable economic development, Japan has been the first country to deal effectively with the problems of pollution.

The other law of thermodynamics, the law of energy, is that the total sum of the material and energy in a given system is fixed, and cannot be spontaneously increased or diminished. Moreover, matter may change in form but not in substance. This is identical with the truth of "voidness" expounded by the Buddha. It can be found in the Sutra of Innumerable Meanings: "All laws [phenomena] were originally, will be, and are in themselves void in nature and form; they are neither great nor small, neither appearing nor disappearing." The Buddha expounded this more than 2,500 years ago, so we can see that in reality he was also a great scientist.

Nevertheless, some Japanese still think of Buddhism as obsolete and irrelevant to the country's prosperity. They ignore its teaching of the wisdom of being satisfied with little. Quite to the contrary, this teaching has great significance for human survival. Now is the time for reaffirming it.

The wisdom of being satisfied with little is the key to both individual and human happiness.

Gratitude

For the past two decades I have devoted myself to the activities of the World Conference on Religion and Peace (WCRP). The WCRP is a group of religious leaders from many countries who work with one spirit for world peace. It has expanded its activities and promotion of step-by-step progress toward world peace to include assistance to developing nations, service as a United Nations nongovernmental organization, and calls for disarmament at the Special Sessions of the UN General Assembly Devoted to Disarmament. The WCRP convenes a substantial world assembly every four years and has had five so far. It has grown into a world organization for inter-religious dialogue, with over 600 participants from 60 nations.

When I reflect on how I have been able to devote what little talent I have to promoting the WCRP, what comes to mind is the help and kindness I have received from a truly wide variety of people. Surrounded by my family and grandchildren and sustained by the assurance of being able to rely on so many people, I can carry out my duties from one day to the next. If I look a little further, I can see that I am sustained by the efforts of kindred spirits not only in Japan but all around the world. I feel this from the bottom of my heart.

Just who was it that created me? Needless to say, it was my father and mother. My father worked hard every day in the fields, was the center of the harmony of our family, and engraved on my heart the importance of a life of honesty. My kind mother strained her frail constitution working constantly at household chores, caring for the silkworms, plying the loom, making good use of the slightest moment of leisure, and sitting at night by the hearth patching our clothing.

Words fail to describe how indebted I am to all the teachers who have instructed me from elementary school to the present day. It was my spiritual mentor, Sukenobu Arai (1879–1949), who opened my eyes to the Lotus Sutra. It is impossible for me to imagine how different I would have been had I not met him. When I think about the great karmic connection that allowed me to meet Arai, I can only put my palms together in a prayer of gratitude.

When we stop to think about it, we realize that we live surrounded by the affection of many people. Of course, there are some who fling malice, hatred, or jealousy at us, but those who touch our lives with warmth and friendship are certainly in the majority. This encompasses not only visible signs of love and words of kindness and encouragement from family and close friends, but also the actions of many people whom we have met only once or twice, or who were once close to us, who are concerned about us from afar and watch over us. When we realize this, there arises in us a feeling of gratitude for even the invisible bonds among human beings.

The woodblock artist Shiko Munakata (1903–75),

who carved out a world all his own, is said to have murmured while engrossed in carving his blocks, "Thank goodness, thank goodness. The chisel is cutting along by itself." To whom was he so grateful? Probably not even he himself knew exactly. Something invisible simply set his carving tools in motion. Somewhere, along the boundary between consciousness and unconsciousness, he felt this invisible force and softly murmured his gratitude. Surely at such a moment Munakata was completely happy.

There is a strong tendency today to give a logical explanation for everything and to deal with things as matters of rights and duties. For example, some people think that when a parent raises a child, the parent is only obeying an animal instinct, so there is no particular reason for the child to be thankful. Some think that it is only natural for teachers to teach, since after all they receive salaries. Pursuing this line of thought, one concludes that plants give oxygen just because they are alive, and that the sun gives light and heat as just a natural phenomenon. In other words, there is no cause to be thankful.

There is no way for such thinking to make people happy. It can only make people egoistic, coldhearted, puffed up, and lonely. By contrast, we cannot imagine how much happier it makes us to be grateful to our parents, to the people around us, to the plant kingdom, and for the blessings of heaven and earth. If the number of people who feel such thankfulness grows into the thousands

and millions, not only will they support one another with affection, but they will be able to exist
in harmony with the plants, the oceans, and the
atmosphere. This planet will become a peaceful,
comfortable place to live.

When one looks at how the world is formed,
one can understand that everything is interdependent, and is connected in some way. Nothing
exists entirely in and of itself. Our environment is
one of constant, interrelated change, in which the
death of one thing becomes the source of life for
another. With everything so interdependent, a
grand but subtle harmony is built up. As a consequence, we can say that it is most natural to live
in grateful acceptance of every encounter with
those who share this bond. Conversely, as long as
we do not forget to see things as they are, the
feeling of gratitude for all things will surely
spring forth.

Happiness comes from the thankfulness we feel as we
become aware of the many earthly and divine bless-
ings we receive, including the support of many other
people.

Looking into the Depths

Each of us meets many people in our daily lives,
and the key to happiness lies in how we relate to
them. If we can practice amicability in relationships with people we meet for the first time, and

also with those we see regularly, then we ought to be that much happier.

A poem by Matsuo Basho (1644–94) reads, "Someone wears a rush mat in a springtime of flowers." The usual interpretation of this poem is that on a beautiful spring day in Kyoto the sight of a beggar wearing a rush mat reminded Basho of the distinguished Zen priest Shuho Myocho (1282–1337), who for twenty years was "combed by the wind" (wandering the country), and Basho thought the man wearing the rush mat might also be a devout priest who had renounced the world. Basho may have had an even more profound insight. He may have sensed something sacred deep in the heart of the mat wearer.

Here is another poem by Basho: "Looking closely, I see a shepherd's purse blooming on the hedge." Sticking out of a common hedge, even the lowly shepherd's purse, a flower one would hardly stop to look at, revealed something of the nobility of life to Basho's eye. In this way of seeing, one does not merely look at a person's surface and decide that they are good or bad. Instead, one looks into a person's depths to find the nobility of life that is linked to the Buddha. When one does this, one discovers respect for the person. The same is true of things. When one stops to wonder why a particular thing exists, one can only assume that the great source of all life causes things to exist as they are. Moreover, when one considers the deep karmic connection that brought the thing into one's hands, one must feel deep love and veneration.

There are undoubtedly some who would say, "What is the point of all this respect?" There may even be some who think that, after all, it is merely idealistic. This, however, is a narrow point of view, and if we lack respect for all things, society will not attain true peace. What would happen if people did not respect others at all? They would think nothing of cheating, intimidating, and harming others, and conflicts would proliferate unabated. If one does not respect others, one cannot trust them. If one cannot trust others, one is always on guard. In such a situation, those with power use it against others; those without power use lies and deception to protect themselves. Neither has a moment of peace.

The same is true of products. Without respect for its products, a manufacturer thinks only of profit. The consumer uses the product and throws it away before it wears out. For example, in Japan one sees abandoned cars along the side of the road, and if this problem grows worse the planet will one day be covered with waste, and people would have no place to live.

I may seem to be going too far, but isn't this the way the world seems to be heading? The reason there is less respect today for people and things is that people look only at the surface of things and do not attempt to see their true value. We tend to judge people only by their academic background, ability, or position, as if to determine whether they might be of benefit to us. Even those who look a little deeper seem to consider only personality—whether someone is friendly and a suitable companion. As long as one judges others only with such an egocentric standard of values, it is impossible to feel true respect.

The reason we are swayed by this shallow way of seeing things is that we are so busy in our daily lives that we have no spiritual breadth. It also seems that there are faults in our education: too much rote memorization, and little attention to teaching students to think for themselves.

It is here, in my opinion, that religion becomes necessary. Religion makes us study things more deeply. It restores our hearts to their original purity. A person with faith venerates all humanity, respects things, and reveres life itself. When people respect one another and physical things, human harmony is created, the relationship between people and things is set right, and peace of mind and happiness result.

In a collection of lectures titled *Kokoro ni Tane o Maku* (Sowing Seeds in the Heart), by Daigaku Hanaoka (1910–88), known for his Buddhist stories for children, we find the following anecdote:

One day I guided a group of young parishioners' wives around Kyoto. Toward evening we decided to eat supper near Kyoto Station and went into an inexpensive restaurant. When the simple meal of chicken and egg on rice was brought, we put our palms together in prayer and began to eat. After we finished our plates without leaving a single bite, we again put our palms together and gave thanks.

When we went to the counter to pay our bill, the fiftyish owner of the restaurant said, "It's not necessary to pay." When we asked why, he replied, "I've been running this restaurant for nearly thirty years now. I've cooked all these years hoping my customers were enjoying the food. But today, for the very first time, someone has shown true gratitude for the simple meal I prepared, and a group of twenty people at that. Nothing could make me happier." Tears welled up in his eyes as he spoke.

I believe that Hanaoka's and his parishioners' gesture of gratitude for a plain meal was merely a natural expression of their Buddhist faith that everything that comes to hand is provided by the Buddha. Whether it is a person or a thing that one is thankful for, putting one's palms together expresses a gratitude that cannot be put into words.

When people begin to greet one another respectfully, a certain warmth inevitably arises. It is not just a matter of form, but rather that, from deep in the heart of the person so greeted, there comes forth something worthy of respect.

Treating all people and things with reverence fills our hearts with harmony, peace, and happiness.

Self-Awareness

Sometimes we allow ourselves to slack off a little because we hear an inner voice saying, "It's all right because no one's looking." At these moments we usually hear another voice, scolding, "Are you really sure it's all right to be doing this?" Occasionally we even hear a voice consoling us, saying, "You sure are working hard." How does this "other self" work?

In Buddhism we have the terms "transient self" and "true self." The former is possessed of the physical body and spirit and is the self that laughs and suffers through daily life. According to Zen, there is also a true self, which existed before our parents gave us life. The true self is a child of the Buddha, imbued at birth with the life of a buddha.

Daisetz Suzuki (1870–1966), who introduced Zen to the West, said, "Within the self there is still another self." He explained that the first self is mutable and the other self is aware of the first. This second self is the essential, or true, self. This is rather difficult terminology, so I refer to the "observed self" and the "seeing self." What is significant is that everyone has this other "seeing self."

Basho wrote this haiku: "My horse plods along through the summer fields; I see myself as in a picture." Basho's horse raises little dust as it plods along without much vigor. Basho places another self a short way away, and this other self watches him sway back and forth on horseback, as in a picture on a scroll. The Basho actually riding the horse is the "observed self." The seeing self can put the observed self in a haiku. This function of the mind is extremely important for a life of virtue.

If insects, fish, birds, or animals have souls, these souls probably consist of their instinct for survival. Of course, humans often follow instinct. Yet humans are also capable of the detachment necessary to be aware of instinct. In other words, the seeing self is separate, and it is what most distinguishes humans from other animals. It is when this seeing self is allowed to function to the full that human beings are most human.

Conscience and introspection are functions of the seeing self. Sometimes we blurt out things that hurt others and do things that cause lasting resentment. For the most part, we do these things when we forget ourselves and lose our temper, but forgetting oneself is treacherous, and it means that one has lost one's seeing self. There are also times when, stepping off the straight road of life, we indulge in pleasures and even perversities, and merely pass our days without cultivating the true nature we are born with. We frequently come to such forks in the road of daily life, and if we can return to ourselves and put the seeing self to work, we can avoid the dangers of the byroads and stick to the true path.

Date Masamune (1567–1636), the great *daimyo* (feudal baron) of the Sendai fief, cherished a certain tea bowl made by a famous potter, and one day as he sat holding it in his hands and admiring it, it slipped from his grasp. Fortunately, it fell in his lap and no damage was done, but when he picked it up, he flung it with all his might against a stone in the garden. Then, turning to his stunned retainers, he laughed and said, "When the tea bowl slipped from my hands, I was startled. For a military commander to be startled by the mere slipping of a tea bowl is extremely embarrassing. I have therefore done away with the source of my embarrassment." In other words, Masamune promptly put his seeing self into action, pulled himself back from turning into the side road, and returned to the main road that was his true self.

Since I was born and raised in Niigata Prefecture, I have a special affection for the Zen priest and poet Ryokan (1758–1831), who was from the same region. Ryokan had a nephew named Umanosuke, who lived with Ryokan's parents and completely abandoned himself to dissolute ways. Whatever anyone said, he would not give up his immoral life, so his friends and relatives went to Ryokan, who was at the hermitage Gogo-an on a nearby mountain. They persuaded him to return to his home village to talk to Umanosuke and try to straighten him out. Ryokan went back home for three days, but in all that time he uttered not a word of rebuke to Umanosuke. As he prepared for the return journey and started to put on his sandals, he couldn't seem to tie them properly. He turned to Umanosuke and asked him to tie the thongs for him. Relieved that Ryokan had said nothing at all during his visit, Umanosuke kneeled down and tied the thongs. But as he was doing this, a teardrop fell on his hand. Startled, he looked up and saw tears running down Ryokan's face. Umanosuke completely gave up his old ways that very day.

Deep inside, however wayward a person might be, he or she is endowed with the buddha-nature (the potential for buddhahood). In this case, Umanosuke was awakened to his buddha-nature by Ryokan's tears of great compassion. From within his dissolute and unruly transient self, his true self rose to the surface. Ryokan was known to appreciate an old poem that asked if one could see into someone's heart by looking them in the eye. Someone whose face shows no trace of sorrow may yet be full of grief. Ryokan undoubtedly saw Umanosuke's grief in his eyes. That was why he prepared to return without a word of rebuke. I think it was when Ryokan felt Umanosuke's troubles as his own that he began to weep.

People may differ about the right way to live, but might we not agree that it amounts to the manifestation of the seeing self? There are many ways of becoming aware of the seeing self, but I believe that in the end they are all found in our relationships with people.

Let your "seeing self" watch over what you say and do, and you will know what is the right thing to do.

EVEN THOUGH YOU BELIEVE
YOU ARE RIGHT

Attitudes Can Easily Change

How does one educate and cultivate oneself as a human being? It is my belief that the most adaptable means of spiritual cultivation is the teachings of Buddhism. It is attitude that makes a person happy or miserable. Since attitude can change, anyone can become happy. That is what Buddhism teaches. Even in the matter of world peace, if the spirit of each individual becomes filled with peace, then the world will of its own accord become peaceful.

Some will say that changing one's attitude in such a way is very difficult. But it is easier to change one's attitude than it is to change matter. Let us say that we have some wood. Even if someone tells us to turn it into iron, there is no way we can comply. However, if someone notices that we are easily angered and suggests that we keep our temper, we would not consider it impossible. We would consider it a definite possibility once we had made up our mind.

Ingen (1592–1673) was the Chinese Zen master who founded the Obaku sect of Zen Buddhism in Japan, and there is a well-known anecdote about him. While traveling along a deserted mountain path, he was suddenly accosted by robbers who threatened him and demanded all his money. Turning his purse upside down, he complied with their demand, saying, "Here is all the money I have," and went on his way. After a short while he returned to where the robbers lay in wait. "Earlier I said that what I gave you was all I had, but then I remembered the gold coin I had received from some parishioners and had tucked into my waistband. Since I have taken the vows of a priest, I cannot tell a lie, so I have returned. Here, please take this coin, too." On hearing these words the highwaymen all fell immediately to their knees and prostrated themselves before the priest. They condemned their old habits, asked to be accepted as disciples, and renounced their worldly lives. The meaning of this story is that although one may not even be trying to change oneself, the heart can easily be transformed by some very small opportunity.

Let's consider another example. From the final days of the Tokugawa shogunate to the early days of the Meiji period, Hara Tanzan (1819–92) was renowned as a Zen priest and served as a superintendent of the main Soto sect academy. He studied Confucianism in his youth at an official academy of the Tokugawa shogunate. Hara was betrayed by a woman with whom he had developed an intimate relationship, and he intruded into her home with the intention of murdering her. She was not at home. Determined to wait until she returned, he flipped through a book that was at hand and his eyes fell on a passage that admonished against sexual passion. As he read on he became unable to bear his own folly. He fled the house and never approached the woman again. He thus avoided the sin of the murder he had intended to commit, and in due course he was able to follow the path of a disciple of the Buddha. His heart changed in an instant because of a book he had just happened to take up.

There are many such examples we might cite. Though attitudes may seem hard to alter, in reality they are easily transformed. Changing the physical, where it is possible, requires considerable effort; changing the spirit can be done in a moment.

Do our actions automatically change when our spirit does? The Chinese thinker Sun Yat-sen held that knowing is difficult but that doing is easy. Normally, we think the opposite is the case; that is, we are convinced that knowing is simple but that doing is difficult. For instance, the great T'ang dynasty poet Po Chü-i once traveled through the West Lake district. Hearing that there was a priest of great virtue named Niao-k'ê who used to practice meditation in a tree in the mountains, Po Chü-i went to meet him. He inquired of the Zen master, "What is the essence of the teachings of the Buddha?" Niao-k'ê replied,

"Do no evil, do all that is good, purify your mind. This is the teaching of all the buddhas." Po Chü-i laughed and said, "Even a child of three can comprehend such a teaching." Niao-k'ê replied, "This can be understood even by a child of three, but it is difficult even for an old man of eighty to practice." Po Chü-i was left speechless and on the spot became a disciple of the Zen master.

This story shows that although one may understand something with one's mind, it is difficult to act on that knowledge. "Be strict with oneself and tolerant with others." "Be calm in adversity; be indifferent in prosperity." "Do what is good for the company." Even though we may understand these exhortations intellectually, there are many things that are not so easy actually to carry out.

Sun Yat-sen, however, claimed that this is not true. He said that doing is much simpler than knowing. Perhaps it is true that once one really understands what one should do, putting it into practice is simple. Moreover, if one doesn't practice, then one really does not understand. I constantly feel that this is the case.

Accordingly, I always hope that many people will be guided in what they do by the valuable teachings of the Lotus Sutra, one of Mahayana Buddhism's most important scriptures. Once they fully understand its teachings, they cannot help changing for the better and naturally following the right path.

The Lotus Sutra teaches that all people may become buddhas. It is because they do not perceive this that they suffer, are tormented, become covetous, quarrel, and head down the wrong road. One of the seven parables in the Lotus Sutra is that of the gem hidden in the robe. A poor man visited the home of a good friend. The friend entertained the poor man cordially with food and drink, and as a result the man got quite drunk and fell asleep. Just then, the friend was called away on some business. Hating to awaken the sleeping man, the friend quickly sewed a priceless jewel into the lining of his friend's clothes and left. When the poor man awoke and found that his friend had gone out, he decided that there was nothing else to do but leave the house, too. He resumed his wretched life of wandering and his struggle for food and clothing, relieved to obtain whatever income he could. A long time passed, and one day the man met his old friend along the road. The friend looked at the man's wretched condition and said, "Such foolishness! On the day we last met I sewed a precious gem into the lining of your clothes so that you would be able to enjoy a comfortable life. But look at you now!" For the very first time the man became aware that he possessed a valuable jewel.

We, too, possess a jewel that we do not take notice of—the priceless jewel of the buddha-nature. If we could only become aware of this, our hearts would change in an instant.

Anyone who really wants to improve their attitude can do so in a moment.

Flexibility of Mind

Is it possible to endow a robot with the common sense of a human being? This has become a subject of great interest in the continuing development of android robots. State-of-the-art robots are said to be superior to humans in terms of memory and data processing. However, if only one aspect of knowledge is emphasized, a robot may also make an extreme judgment, such as that it is acceptable to kill people for the sake of peace. For a safety valve to check such recklessness, we have discovered the necessity of some kind of common sense or emotion. Nevertheless, endowing a robot with common sense has proved extremely difficult. A systems engineering professor at Hosei University, Toshiro Terano, explains, "This is because common sense is the accumulation of human knowledge over thousands of years."

To see clearly the true cause of all events, that is, the origin of existence, is to possess genuine common sense. A famous phrase in the Lotus Sutra, "in character upright, in mind gentle," refers to someone who is honest and flexible enough always to accept the truth; in other words, someone with flexibility of mind.

To understand the importance of flexibility, let us observe the functioning of the hand. We can see that unless the wrist and fingers are able to move supply, one cannot improve, for example, one's playing of the piano or violin. The same is true of needlework, handicrafts, and artwork. If the body is not limber, then it is doubtful whether one can improve one's skill in baseball, wrestling, judo, or any physical activity. The reason for this is that if the arm, the hip, or the wrist is not supple, then it will not be able to move in the way it is supposed to in theory.

Spiritual flexibility is even more important. Christ said, "Blessed are the meek; for they shall inherit the earth." This may be taken to mean that one who is flexible enough to accept the truth can build a new world.

It seems that, in many cases, once people reach a certain position in life, they become self-righteous. They are dogmatic about their own ideas, position, or appearances, and are unable to change. In disputes between individuals as well as nations, a deadlock occurs when people are so attached to their own beliefs or positions that they lack the breadth of mind to make mutual concessions. Just how much this inflexibility hinders the progress of societies and human happiness is hard to measure.

Dr. Sakuzo Yoshino (1878–1933), a professor of political science at the University of Tokyo and an advocate of Japan's prodemocracy movement in the early twentieth century, wrote a book concerning his expectations of his students. He wrote that while it was important for them to seek out the truth and advocate their principles, it often happened that once they became convinced of a truth, they tended to close their minds to other approaches. "What I want most of my students," he wrote, "is openness to truth. . . . The student's approach to the quest for truth must be not only passionate, but also inconsistent. To prevent misunderstanding, let me explain what I mean by *inconsistent*. I mean that students must constantly strive to be right and that they must be prepared to change their minds if the need arises." This is flexibility of mind.

Undoubtedly, some would reject Dr. Yoshino's view, saying it might be all right for students, whose role is to pursue the truth, to be inconsistent, but that people in positions of responsibility cannot afford that. Normally, we think that inconsistency means a willingness to compromise under pressure. But Dr. Yoshino advocates inconsistency in the sense of honesty, bravery, and open-mindedness, which are essential for progress.

Inability to make that kind of headway is caused by preoccupation with appearances, which have absolutely nothing to do with essential qualities. In adhering to such meaningless things and hesitating to take a first step even though one has discovered the right path, one is unable to rid oneself of delusion, and leaves others trapped in delusion as well. Nothing could be more foolish.

Oneself and one's family, work, position, and belongings—all are important. However, when one is freed from these self-centered fetters, a larger world opens up. If one is liberated from these things, the heart becomes lighter and invigorated, and one begins to live for others. How may one be liberated from such captivity? Yamamoto Tsunetomo (1659–1719) wrote in *Hagakure* (In the Shadow of Leaves), a book on the way of the samurai, that one does this by dying. But that will not do.

There is a delightful story about Zen Master Fugai Honko (1779–1847) and a horsefly. When Fugai was the priest of a deteriorating temple in Osaka, a wealthy merchant came to talk with him about problems that weighed heavily on his mind. Fugai showed absolutely no interest in the man's plight, but instead watched intently as a horsefly flew against the window and fell to the floor. Again and again it flew against the window and fell. The merchant could bear it no longer and said sarcastically, "The Reverend seems extremely fond of horseflies." In reply Fugai mumbled, "That horsefly seems fully determined to go out that window. Although this dilapidated temple has big holes everywhere, it keeps flinging itself against the window, convinced that it's the only way out. But it is not only the horsefly that is to be pitied."

Everyone believes that their way of thinking is right. One needs that sort of confidence, but if one becomes enslaved to it, one misses out on a larger world. By humbly admitting that there might be other, better approaches, one is freed of such entrapment.

I would like to recount another story, about Eisai (1141–1215), the founder of the Rinzai sect of Japanese Buddhism. A poor man came to the temple Eisai founded in Kyoto, Kennin-ji, and entreated Eisai, "My family has had nothing to eat for many days. My wife and three children are on the verge of starvation. Please help us." As things would have it, however, the temple was also very poor and there was nothing to give the man. By chance, however, some copper was left over from the nimbus of a statue of the Buddha Yakushi (Medicine Master), and Eisai gave it to the man and told him to trade it for food. Later some disciples expressed doubts about the propriety of giving the man something as important as a piece of a buddha. Eisai replied, "In one of his previous incarnations as a bodhisattva, did not the Buddha cut the flesh of his own body to feed sentient beings? Would it not be in keeping with his intentions if we gave the entire statue to help people dying of starvation? If I am cast into hell for committing this sin, then so be it. I am only eager to save the starving."

Each time we cease to be consumed by something, we become able to see a better and more correct path. It is by these means that compassion overflows. When we persist in defending only one view, do we not lose sight of the path of universal truth, which gives life to both ourselves and others?

Each of us always ought to cultivate the flexibility of mind that is prepared to part with the "small self." If only we do that, the true path will of its own accord come into view and we will be able to follow it meekly. And true salvation will be consummated.

The rewards of being flexible enough to accept unpleasant truths include spiritual growth for the individual, and social progress for the community.

Desires in the Service of Virtue

As Japan has come to assume a greater role in international affairs, its people have placed greater importance on ability in foreign languages and on professional knowledge and skills. These are indisputably significant, but does it not seem that there is something even more important, namely the possession of a certain "mirror" with which one can view one's way of life?

We have various desires: to be found sexually attractive, to obtain a better lifestyle, to succeed in business, to attain positions of honor and distinction, to raise our children to be respectable members of society. Desires such as these—for self-improvement—are manifold and entirely reasonable. However, if one becomes enslaved to such desires, then one may lose sight of the right way to live. Therefore one must be extremely cautious.

The delusions that lie concealed in the depths of the human heart are not easily extinguished. The eminent, virtuous priest Saicho (767–822), finding this to be the case, humbly referred to himself as "Low-down Saicho," and a holy man like Honen (1133–1212) disparaged himself as "Grumbling Honen." This self-awareness in and of itself is priceless. Too often those who are conceited enough to think themselves virtuous never improve spiritually.

If we were to negate all human desires, we would be left with a mere shell of humanity. Buddhism says that human beings possess 108 delusions, so even if one hoped to make a clean sweep of them all, it would be well-nigh impossible. On the contrary, one's whole spirit might be caught up in the impossible task, and one would find oneself in a great predicament. Yet Mahayana Buddhism teaches that these same delusions are means for progress along the road to enlightenment. For example, while the agony of lost love may drive one person to heavy drinking, it may lead another to write a superior novel. Aggressive enterprise may lead a person either to break the law or to contribute to a whole nation's prosperity.

Now then, how might these delusions be put to good use? I believe that the foundation for this may be found in the Eightfold Path preached by the Buddha. Following his enlightenment, the Buddha first expounded the Dharma to the five ascetics in Deer Park, at Sarnath, and preached the Eightfold Path, consisting of right view, right thinking, right speech, right action, right living, right endeavor, right memory, and right meditation. If one set out to practice all eight from the very beginning, one would very soon abandon the attempt as impossible. As a first step, let us consider putting the first three into practice. As one endeavors to see, think, and speak rightly, the remaining five naturally follow along in good order.

The terms "right" and "rightly" mean thinking and behaving in ways consistent not only with reason and ethics but with the two truths "All things are impermanent" and "Nothing has an ego."

"All things are impermanent" means that everyone and everything is constantly changing. The sun and the innumerable other heavenly bodies are incessantly metamorphosing; the subatomic particles that constitute all matter change from moment to moment. Neither our bodies nor our environment are exempt from this law of change. For example, Japan's lifetime employment system, so often pointed to as a special feature of Japanese companies, is slowly undergoing a change. More and more workers change jobs in pursuit of work where they may make better use of their abilities, and even large corporations have begun to hire people in midcareer. Furthermore, there are continuous changes in management styles, from a stress on applied technology to an emphasis on basic technology, from the pursuit of efficiency to a quest for creativity.

"Nothing has an ego" means that all things are interconnected and that nothing exists entirely in and of itself. If you but reflect for a moment, you will immediately recognize this to be true—from the movement of the stars in the heavens to your own small existence.

If one will see and think of things "rightly," in accordance with these two truths, then one will never be mistaken. If one cannot establish this foundation, then one will merely cling to the self and end up seeing everything with oneself as the center. Thus engrossed in self-interest, one will succumb to selfish desires, want more and more, fall into frustration, behave according to whims, and cause annoyance to everyone.

If one does become able to see and think in accordance with these truths—"All things are impermanent" and "Nothing has an ego"—then one will not be inclined toward the self-centered way of life. One will be able to see oneself objectively, and in the light of the surrounding phenomena one will be able to see into one's heart.

The Buddha once asked his son, Rahula, "Why do you think people look at themselves in the mirror?" Rahula replied, "I believe they want to see the pure and the impure, the good and evil aspects of their own faces." The Buddha nodded his approval of Rahula's reply and warned, "That is true. Just as one looks at the purity and impurity of one's face reflected in a mirror, it is important that human beings themselves observe that which is done by their bodies, mouths, and hearts."

It is only by the act of observing, as if looking at one's reflection in a mirror, the way in which the body behaves, the words one utters, and the thoughts one thinks that one obtains the key to a better life. If one does this, the wretchedness of selfish desires will be reflected in that mirror, and one will judiciously bring them under control and endeavor to change them into something more pleasant. This is the road to purifying the soul; this is the practice by which one can change delusions into a force for good.

Rather than try to rid ourselves of delusions, we should examine them carefully and consider how to make good use of them.

If You Think
You Are the Most Important

Scientific and technological progress has made Japan incomparably more prosperous and convenient than it was half a century ago. Nevertheless, it does seem that our view of the world has become singularly self-centered.

People tend to think that the self is the most important thing, but in reality they do not seem to be taking such good care of that self. Rather, there seem to be more people who are wasting the precious self, perhaps because they think that the self is merely the physical body, so the best way to live is to fulfill one's desires. However, the true self is hardly so insignificant.

The Buddha justifiably did not disparage self-esteem. A collection of short sutras quotes him as saying:

> The whole wide world we traverse with our thoughts,
> And nothing that man finds is more dear than self.
> Since the self is so very dear to others,
> Those who know the love of self
> Must harm no other man.

The lesson here is that those who love themselves must love others. If one would live in a way that sets great store by the self, then one should not think only of one's own self, but earnestly value the self of others.

It may appear that as we take care of ourselves we absolutely ignore others. To the contrary, there are many who go through life envying, resenting, and showing enmity toward others. They are hardly taking care of themselves in the long run. What they are doing is wasting the self. It may sound paradoxical, but if one really places a high value on oneself, then one will love others.

Gempo Yamamoto (1866–1961) was known as the modern Hakuin (1685–1768), after the priest who revitalized Rinzai Zen Buddhism. A certain person came to him and complained of being too weak to work. Yamamoto admonished him severely, saying, "It is not that you lack strength. What you lack is virtue." Whenever Yamamoto stayed at an inn he would arrange fellow travelers' slippers at the bath entrance and even fold their nightwear and bedding for them, constantly performing unnoticed acts of kindness. This is what is meant by having a high regard for yourself and the people around you.

Japan's feudal period was one of obedience to authority. In contrast, the age of democracy may be characterized as one of understanding and cooperation. And it is said that the final age of human society will be one of loving others and respecting harmony. This is not to say that such an age will simply happen; rather, it is up to us to establish it.

Mahatma Gandhi once said that he believed that what is possible for one person is possible for all. It may be that loving others is something only a very few people can devote themselves to. Yet, however few such people may be, since there are some who can leap into that elevated sphere, it must be possible for everyone. Hence I would like to propose that self-love be broadened little by little.

Even those who feel that they have their hands full just thinking about themselves should try to give similar consideration to their own parents and brothers and sisters. This is comparatively easy to accomplish. There are, of course, homes where even this cannot be done and which are filled with rancor, but if one simply allows oneself to be kind, then one will naturally be as considerate of friends and colleagues as of family members. With an open heart accept their self-love, endeavoring to develop relationships in which one can share both their joys and sorrows. This is surely hard to accomplish at a single swoop, but one can put it into practice one small opportunity at a time.

Next, expand your concern to the town where you live. For example, you can tidy up the small park near your home, or if you see that the gutters are filled with mud, talk the situation over with others and work together to clean them. In this way, gradually extending the parameters of self-love soon becomes a habit, and your concern will extend to encompass all of society. Just to give another small example, if you go into a lavatory on a train and find the rim of the toilet bowl dirty, wipe it for the next person. To give a larger example, you might contribute to or take part in a campaign to help refugees or plant trees. The sphere of your active concern will expand and deepen.

Were self-love to open outward, the joy and sadness of all humankind would meld with one's own. If there were an increase in the number of those who could not distinguish between others' feelings and their own, then surely the ideal society of love and harmony would be right before our eyes.

If you are convinced that you must rid yourself of self-centeredness, you will probably feel resigned and tell yourself you simply cannot. As the Buddha said, we must recognize that others also have self-esteem and identify with it. If you first try to be of even small service to others, you will feel good. To that degree your heart will be cleansed. As you come to feel pleasure in making others happy, you will gradually cease to be self-centered. As you widen your concern to a broader world, your self-centeredness will, on its own, fade away.

Broaden your self-love to love for your family, the people in your community, and finally all humanity.

Ask Yourself, "Is This All Right?"

Over a decade ago the Japanese Committee of the World Conference on Religion and Peace (WCRP/Japan) invited Mother Teresa, the 1979 Nobel Peace Prize recipient, to Japan to commemorate the first decade of the WCRP. In her keynote speech she said, "The children of Japan are delightful, but the adults seem too fidgety and are lacking something spiritual. There are too few smiling faces, and expressions are gloomy." I remember being struck by this comment. Perhaps she saw that despite our country's affluence, we are constantly on guard, looking out for what may be advantageous to us.

I believe Japan is today the most affluent nation in the world. Japan's rate of unemployment, despite a slight rise to about 3 percent, is low compared with the rate of 10 percent in several European countries. If young Japanese were less fastidious about desiring high wages and easy work, the unemployment rate would possibly be even lower. Businesses that have adopted the two-day weekend are on the increase, and there is almost an overabundance of leisure facilities. College students can enjoy overseas travel on money earned from part-time jobs.

However, is it really all right to take the current situation for granted? I can't help worrying that eventually we will face a day of reckoning. Even without one, I believe human progress will be impeded if we merely drag our feet through daily life, presuming that this blessed environment will continue indefinitely.

There are many sides to what we call human progress, and what I want to stress here is spiritual progress. Humanity has made tremendous spiritual progress in recognizing that the right to pursue happiness belongs not only to individuals, families, and other small groups, but also to ever larger numbers of people. Sometimes such progress carries the cost of individual self-sacrifice and pain. However, unless one is unafraid of pain and decides to devote oneself to some kind of action, happiness for humanity as a whole will remain out of reach.

What I want to propose here is that you constantly ask yourself, "Is this all right?"—that is, that you continually question in your own mind, "Is the present condition of the world acceptable?" "Is it all right for people in this country to be this way?" "Is my own lifestyle all right the way it is?" If you do this, a variety of uncertainties and doubts appear, like clouds in the sky. To resolve these, you must initiate some form of action.

What action should one take? The first, which seems commonplace enough, is endeavoring to improve oneself; that is, making an effort to take one step forward spiritually, physically, and in the ability to act. Those with a proper worldview will be dissatisfied with that alone, because they know that they will not thrive unless many others are saved materially and spiritually and enjoy happiness. At that point there naturally arises a desire to advance together with everyone else.

A story is told about Albert Schweitzer when he was a young student. He was at home on vacation, and one morning as he gazed at the beautiful early-summer garden outside his window, he was filled with happiness. He contemplated his happiness in being blessed with two kind parents and in being able to devote his time to his favorite studies and to playing the organ. At that very moment, however, a doubt flitted through his mind: Was this the way things should be? Outside his window a small bird continued to chirp. By and by, the words of Jesus Christ came to mind: "By gaining his life a man will lose it; by losing his life for my sake, he will gain it" (Matt. 10:39). At that moment he felt something like a revelation seize his entire body. After a moment's contemplation Schweitzer made a pledge in his heart: "Until the age of thirty I shall live for scholarship and art and then I shall devote what remains of my life to the service of humanity." In that instant the course of his life was decided.

On graduating from university, Schweitzer served as a minister and university lecturer and continued playing the organ, a talent which he had exhibited early in life, becoming a man of distinction. On learning that many people in Africa were dying from lack of medical treatment, he decided to carry out the pledge of his earlier days by practicing medicine in Africa. He audited classes in medical care at his alma mater, the University of Strasbourg, and at the age of thirty-eight went to the province of Gabon in French Equatorial Africa and opened a hospital at Lambaréné. In the fiercely hot, humid jungle, where epidemics were rampant, Dr. Schweitzer devoted his life to advancing medical treatment in Africa, saved innumerable lives, and lived to be ninety.

Schweitzer's activities in his later years, which were lauded around the world, commenced that summer morning in his youth when he asked himself whether things were as they should be.

The most highly developed nations' way of life is rapidly depleting natural resources and energy supplies. This is the road that takes the human race toward destruction. Unless people of spirit ask themselves whether this is acceptable, and spare no effort to change the way they live, humanity will ultimately be beyond saving.

Since one person alone can never be happy as long as

many others are unhappy, we must always ask ourselves whether the status quo is all right.

THE ELEPHANT STEPS FIRMLY

What Kind of Flower Is Yours?

In one's thirties one is in the prime of life. A company prospers through the efforts of employees in their thirties who support the section chiefs and department heads, who are in their forties and fifties. The dramatist Zeami (1363–1443) wrote in his *Fushi Kaden* (The Transmission of the Flower of Acting Style) that Noh actors reach the peak of their career at the age of thirty-four or thirty-five:

> For if during these years the actor thoroughly studies the fine points of dramatics and masters the mysteries of his art, he will no doubt become known for his mastery and acquire fame. If at this time society's approval is not forthcoming and he does not attain the reputation he aspires to, however skillful he eventually becomes he must know that his blossom has not yet reached its glory.

Someone who works hard in their teens and

twenties will surely bloom in their thirties. However, Zeami says above that even though you have perfected your professional skills, if the people around you do not recognize it, you have not yet become the genuine article.

Every opportunity I have to speak to young people, I tell them they should try to be "number one" at their place of work. Some may think this is expecting the impossible, but it is not. All one has to do is become the very best at something. This is not restricted to the young; it is equally important for people in middle age. "When it comes to knowing products, that's the person to go to." "If you need some calculating done, she's the best." "When it comes to dealing with whole-salers, he's your man." "For straightening out difficulties, that person is tops." Even such matters of skill will do. Or it might be a matter of character. "If it's serious, he's your man." "She's tops when it comes to persevering." "When it comes to kindness, no one is kinder." In any case, it is important to try to be the best at something. If you can be above average in even one thing, you will feel more confident. That becomes a source of strength. Once you have set your sights on what you want to accomplish and devote all your energy to it, your true worth will become apparent.

Many years ago the critic Daizo Kusayanagi expressed a concern that society had entered an age of "low hurdles," in which most people were lowering the hurdles they had to jump over and were satisfied to do so. Although they thought they were making full use of their potential, they were putting out only 60 to 70 percent. One can hardly expect growth in such a situation.

Each person makes some kind of effort in their life. For those of us who live in society and hold jobs to earn a living, that is perfectly natural. The degree of effort depends on our determination to use uncompromisingly whatever strengths we possess, in order to grow in our jobs and achieve breadth and depth as human beings. Moreover, when we throw ourselves heart and soul into one particular thing, we cultivate honesty and confidence.

If we broaden our vision further, we discover that our various endeavors are intricately tied together in the mesh we call society. Since many people in society contribute and render service to everyone else by doing better than average and more than is expected, society blossoms, filling with vitality, exuberance, inspiration, and a sense of purpose.

Everyone has some ability that is beyond the ordinary. There may be some who lament that they do not, but they are mistaken. The simple fact is that they have not developed their potential.

In the Buddha's time there was in India a powerful kingdom called Kosala. Its queen, Mallika, was of common origin, and as a young girl she worked in a flower garden where hair ornaments were made. One day while Pasenadi, the young king of Kosala, was walking in the garden, he happened to notice Mallika and asked her for water to rinse his feet. The lukewarm water she brought soothed his feet. The king then asked for water to wash his face. This time she brought water that was slightly cool, and it felt very refreshing on his face. Increasingly delighted, the king then asked for water to quench his thirst. The water that Mallika brought to him was very cold, and pleasing to the throat. When the king inquired into the matter, she replied, "The water for your feet was from the surface of the spring, warmed by the sun's rays. The water for your face was from lower down, and the water for you to drink was from the depths." The king promptly decided that she was just the one to be his wife, and he took her to his castle and made her queen of Kosala.

Everyone knows that the temperature of a body of water varies according to the depth, but only someone unusually considerate would use that knowledge to please someone. Because Mallika was that kind of person, she found unexpected happiness.

Shigenobu Okuma (1838–1922), the founder of Waseda University and twice prime minister of Japan, is said to have had poor handwriting. When he was young his calligraphy teacher was a useless drunkard and did not teach his pupil well, and Okuma took a dislike to writing. He completed his studies at the Saga fief school, the Kodokan, and went on to a school of the Dutch and English languages in Nagasaki. He so disliked writing that he took no notes of the lectures, but instead did his best to remember them. This strengthened his memory, and later as a politician he never forgot even the most complicated discussion. This is an example of a man who developed his skill through his own efforts.

Another example is of Kiyoshi Ichimura (1900–1968), the founder of the Ricoh-San-Ai conglomerate, known as an "idea president" and a master of management. Shortly after World War II, several years after he started out in business, he spotted a large plot of vacant land in the Ginza district of central Tokyo, and repeatedly asked the elderly woman who owned it to sell it to him, but she always refused, saying she could not part with land that had always been in her family. Undaunted, Ichimura continued to call on her. Deciding to refuse him once and for all, she went to call on him at his office. The day was cold and sleeting. When she arrived at the office, a young female employee greeted her with a smile and politely offered her slippers to change into. These were ordinary courtesies. But the young woman also took out her handkerchief and wiped the hem of the older woman's kimono, which was wet from the sleet. The old woman was impressed by such thoughtfulness and decided that she liked the kind of company that would hire such employees. She changed her mind on the spot and told Ichimura she would sell him the land. The young woman was unusually consider-

ate. Her kindness and the way in which she received visitors contributed greatly to the company's future.

*Knowing and developing your own special talent will
give you confidence and a sense of strength.*

What Will Light Up Our Hearts?

People should cherish ideals and goals. If they do
not, they quickly succumb to compromises, try to
avoid hardship, and drift with the current. In my
youth the word *ambition* was often heard, and
most young men recited to themselves a poem by
Shaku Gessho (1817–58) that went, "Setting an
aim in life, a young man leaves home, determined
to succeed or never return." It seems that today
status seeking remains but ambition has been forgotten. Since that word has fallen out of favor, it
seems that we have also ignored the words
"pride" and "dignity."

The poet Hideo Yoshino (1902–67) has something significant to say about ambition in "So-
liloquy of a Poet" in his collection of essays
Yawarakana Kokoro (The Tender Heart): "In com-
posing poetry, one must be bold. By this I mean
bold enough to let oneself go and focus sharply
on one thing; poetry requires that spirit. . . . The
true essence of a poem comes from a pliant soul
experiencing an irrepressible feeling and allowing it to find a breach and pour forth." Yoshino

does not use the word *ambition*, but when he refers to his poems' quality of inevitability, it is obvious that is what he is talking about. If one throws oneself into one's work wholeheartedly, then the quality of each day's work will be subtly transformed. Our work will be different from that of others. At first the difference may be slight, but it will gradually become more obvious, and then it will become the kind of work that sparkles and shines, and one will become bold.

Ideals are similar in that they rise high above reality. There is no such thing as an ideal that is not lofty. For example, the Buddhist ideal is to perfect oneself like the Buddha and make this world the Pure Land. Most will say, "That's just beyond the realm of possibility," and give up. There are also people who would probably say, "No matter how hard I try as a single individual, the world will not change."

When we consider the disgraceful conflicts and terrible disasters that frequently occur in our own society, and that so many people on this earth are exposed to the terror of nuclear weapons, scorched by the flames of war, and faced with starvation, the transformation of this world into the Pure Land and the achievement of world peace do seem utterly impossible. That, however, is a misunderstanding of what an ideal is. It stems from the false impression that an ideal is only valid if it is realized.

The ideal of world peace is like a great ocean, and our individual activities are like small drops of water that fall on a tree in a forest in the mountains. One drop provides the earth with a drop of moisture. If enough drops fall, the trees will grow and there will be ground water. Where the ground water emerges as a spring, it will sustain birds and animals, and quench the thirst of the passing traveler. Farther on, it will become a mountain stream, making beautiful ravines and giving fish a place to grow. As it goes farther, it will give life to the crops of the fields that provide human beings with food to eat, and it will provide an important means of transport. Thus water, even before it reaches the great ocean, fulfills a number of definite roles at each stage. Even one drop of water has that much power.

In Japan as elsewhere, there are large numbers of people engaged in volunteer work to improve society and contribute to peace. These people render service at social welfare facilities, raise money for refugees in Asia and Africa, and in general try to add individual drops of water to the oceanic idea of world peace. Through this day-by-day individual effort, the ideal is for certain being accomplished.

Everyone knows the story of Isaac Newton seeing the apple fall and discovering the law of gravity, but his was not a case of sudden enlightenment. Before that chance event, he had long been pondering Kepler's theories of the motions of the planets. When the apple fell, an inspiration flashed through his mind. Moreover, it is said that it took him sixteen years to explicate his discovery. The story of the apple has been emphasized so much that we tend to lose sight of the fact that his great discovery resulted from long, accumulated effort.

When Newton was a young boy he was apparently poor at his studies, but liked to build models. One day he built a scale model of a water mill and showed it to his classmates at school. The mill worked, but when one of the best students asked why the mill could grind grain into flour, he was at a loss for a reply. The classmate said, "If you can't explain why, then it just proves that you are merely clever with your hands," and laughed in derision, giving Newton a painful kick in the side. Unable to forget his chagrin, Newton from then on gave much thought to why things happened. It was because he developed this habit over many years that he became a great scientist.

In 1970, at the first assembly of the World Conference on Religion and Peace in Kyoto, the chairman of the plenary session, Dr. Dana McLean Greeley (1908–86), delivered the keynote address, and a story he told remains in my memory even now, after more than twenty years. In ancient Greece a traveler stopped a local villager and asked how far it was to Mount Olympus, the home of the gods, and how he might get there. The villager thought for a moment and answered, "Mount Olympus is a long way from here, and to get there you head in that direction and walk a step at a time. That's the only way to get there."

In daily life a lot happens to us. If we look only

at our feet we are apt to walk in zigzags. We may even lose our way entirely. Yet if we stick to our ideals we will not lose our way, but progress straight toward our destination. With confidence in our stride, we will go steadily forward a step at a time.

Ideals are worthy not only in themselves, but also for what we learn as we approach them a step at a time.

The Right Length of a Meal

There is a saying, "If you want something done, ask someone who is busy." It might seem more logical to ask someone who is not busy, but such a person is often neglectful. There are many books of advice for businessmen and others on how to manage time and make the most of the twenty-four hours of the day, but I would like to take a slightly different approach.

Some people say they are simply too busy for community service, the peace movement, or their faith. They have convinced themselves that time is an absolute, that there are only twenty-four hours in a day and sixty minutes in an hour, and that nothing can change this. The Lotus Sutra tells of the bodhisattvas who were so engrossed for eons by the Buddha Sun Moon Light's preaching of the Sutra of the Lotus Flower of the Wonderful Law that the time seemed as short as the time it took to eat. The phrase in the Lotus Sutra is "listening to the Buddha's preaching and deeming it but the length of a meal." In other words, time is relative.

The same is true of space flight. According to the theory of relativity, if astronauts traveled away from the earth at slightly less than the speed of light for 2,500 years, what on earth would appear to be 2,500 years would be for the astronauts only a fifty-year period. If a newborn child had set off in a rocket at the time of the birth of the Buddha, it would now be an adult turning fifty. Such an incredible situation is theoretically possible. Even without resorting to such a difficult theory, I am certain that everyone must have had the experience in daily life of time seeming short. Half a day laughing and talking in pleasant company seems to pass in a flash, but a boring day feels very long. An unpleasant task that you do not want to do takes hours and hours, but it is easy to make headway with a pleasant task in a very short time. Time seems long or short depending on one's attitude.

Nichiren (1222–82) was the most discipline-oriented Japanese Buddhist priest, and sought a way to human salvation based on the Lotus Sutra. In 1261, while he was in exile at Ito on the Izu Peninsula, he wrote in his *Shion-sho* ("The Four Debts of Gratitude"—that is, to our parents, rulers, all living things, and the Three Treasures):

For over 240 days, from the twelfth day of the fifth month of last year [when this exile began] to the sixteenth of the first month of this year [today], I have been able day and night to practice the teachings of the Lotus Sutra. Because for the sake of the Lotus Sutra I am placed in this situation [exile], whatever I do—whether I am walking, standing, sitting, or lying—I live by the sutra daily with my whole self. What greater joy than this could there be for someone born human in this world? . . . [Exiled like this] I in effect read the sutra even though I do not remember it, and live by it automatically even though I do not read it.

Just before this passage, Nichiren confesses that for the previous six or seven years, though he had earnestly believed in the Lotus Sutra, he had been preoccupied with study or worldly affairs, and that he had been able to devote time each day to reading only one chapter or chanting the title of the Lotus Sutra (the *daimoku*). Of course, throughout those years Nichiren must have spent twenty-four hours a day with the Lotus Sutra. Yet placed in the special situation of exile, he became palpably aware of his devotion to the Lotus Sutra, and experienced a fullness of the soul that he had not previously known.

I myself have felt that most poignantly. After Rissho Kosei-kai was established, for example, I had not a moment of my own. Though I had gone to bed at two in the morning, I would have to get up at four to make my rounds delivering milk. No sooner had I returned home for breakfast than someone would come and ask me to visit their seriously ill neighbor. I would hurriedly finish breakfast and then go to the sick person's bedside to chant the sutra. After he or she improved, I would return home only to find a large number of believers awaiting me. It was always like that.

Amazingly, being so busy never seemed to me the least bit hard. That is, the Buddha was not giving me a moment's rest, and when I realized that, I truly felt my courage grow a hundredfold. When Nichiren writes, "I live by the sutra daily with my whole self. What greater joy than this could there be for someone born human in this world?" I believe it is this state of mind he means, this momentary sense of the fullness of life.

The great English painter of water and seas, Joseph Mallord Turner (1775–1851), once went to a lake with some friends. He sat on the bank all day gazing at the water. From time to time he would throw a pebble into the water and like a child marvel at the ripples it caused. A friend asked him, "You're always grumbling that you are so busy you don't have enough time to paint, then you come all the way out to the lake here and don't paint at all. Why not?" Turner replied, "True, I have not painted today, but I've been sitting here looking out over the lake. I have learned a lot about the ripples, the light, and the changing of the colors. Rather than make sketches, I have spent the day quite memorably." In other words, Turner's spirit burned at its very brightest on that day.

That is the way time is. Some people live eighty years and their lives are very uninteresting. Others live only thirty and their lives are substantial and full. There is all the difference of heaven and earth between one day passed meaninglessly and one day lived to the full.

Attitude determines whether the time seems long or short and whether we make full use of it.

"All Work Is the Buddha's Work"

Everyone realizes that it is important to be deeply immersed in something. But some people take it into their heads to do first one thing and then another, and end up obtaining nothing at all. That is truly regrettable, because if they could just live their lives absorbed in one interest they would be able to accomplish great things.

I have heard that there is a saying in America, "Never buy a car made on a Monday." Apparently, there is a greater chance that a lemon with loose nuts and bolts will be produced on a Monday, because workers tend to slack off after the weekend. Slackness is not, of course, limited to the United States. The commentator Naoki Komuro wrote in his *Sobieto Teikoku no Hokai* (The Collapse of the Soviet Empire):

In the Soviet Union when one purchases a household appliance, one always tries to select one certified to have been made during the first half of the month. If it is made in the first half, you can rest assured that it was not made in a rush. You can assume it will work. But if it was made in the latter half of the month, there is a possibility that it will fall apart rather quickly.

The Russian worker thinks only of achieving the assigned quota, so in the first half of the month he works slowly. Then, in the second half, he hurries under pressure to reach the quota. Everyone knows the situation, so they try to buy the "early half" products.

The Americans' slipshod method and the Russians' rushed way of manufacturing show a common lack of enthusiasm for factory work. Without dedication, good workmanship can hardly be expected.

Japanese people are rather disposed to concentrate on their work. That Japanese products—cars, cameras, and televisions, for instance—are known to be efficient, unlikely to break down, and long-lasting is because of workers' dedication. This may be partly a national trait, and I think the influence of Buddhism is significant. Buddhism places great emphasis on *samadhi*, remaining tranquil whatever happens and focusing one's thoughts on a single object. Though it was originally a Buddhist ascetic practice, Mahayana Buddhism teaches its application in all aspects of daily life, including work and study.

The Japanese most noted for advocating the

application of *samadhi* in daily life was Suzuki Shosan (1579–1655), a learned priest of the Soto Zen sect who served under Tokugawa Ieyasu. In the section "The Daily Business of Farmers" of his moral essay *Bammin Tokuyo* (For the Benefit of All), Shosan writes:

> Heaven set farmers the vital task of nourishing the world and its people. If they work their farms in diligent accordance with the Way of Heaven, with no thought of themselves; if they produce the five grains and worship the Buddha and the gods; if they make a great vow to save lives and provide enough food even for the insects; if they invoke the name of Amida Buddha each time they sink their hoes in the ground; if they put their hearts into each stroke of their scythes: then the fields in which they labor will be holy ground, and the grain they produce will be holy food. For those who eat it, it will be like a medicine that dispels and vanquishes delusion.

If they invoke the name of Amida with each stroke of the hoe or scythe, they will not be distracted and will be able to concentrate; they will be in a state of profound meditation as they work.

In another section, "The Daily Business of Artisans," Shosan writes:

> A craftsman said to me, "I know it is important to seek the Buddha's wisdom, but I am too busy at my hereditary occupation to do that.

How can I ever hope to achieve buddhahood?"

I replied, "All work is the Buddha's work. It is enough if you find buddhahood in the pursuit of your occupation. You must realize that whatever work you do is work that you are doing for the sake of others. . . . The Eternal Buddha divides himself into ten billion parts in order to benefit the world.

This is a truly wise perspective. You are one of those parts, and your work is the work of the Buddha. You do it to benefit the whole world. All work, of whatever nature, is the Buddha's work, and you can find buddhahood through the diligent pursuit of your occupation. All who throw themselves into their work with a desire to be of service to others will surely resemble the Buddha. Moreover, with the conviction in your heart that you are part of the Buddha and therefore doing the Buddha's work, you will naturally come to concentrate on it.

I believe it was Chekhov who said, "A human being must work. He must work by the sweat of his brow. Therein lies the significance, the purpose, the happiness, the joy, and the deep emotion of human life." As the amount of leisure time in developed countries grows, the number of working hours is decreasing. That is all the more reason why this degree of concentration on the job is important. If one simply tries to get through one's quota, one is bound to end up producing the equivalent of a "Monday car." Someone who falls into the habit of working that way will pass the weekend unenthusiastically as well, whether playing sports or reading. If one only halfheartedly works and plays, then one's entire life will be filled with indifference.

The potter Kanjiro Kawai (1890–1966) once said, "Work is the work of doing work." We are apt to feel proud of the amount of work we accomplish. Priding ourselves on our own accomplishments is important, but good work is the kind that does itself. People find it very hard to accomplish anything truly exceptional by themselves. At work we encounter people we do not get along with. We suffer and endure. We exert our utmost strength. With an invisible strength pushing us onward, we complete one job after another. Rather than boasting, "I did it," we should say, "The work is getting done all by itself; I'm just an assistant." When you really put yourself into your work, you develop this sort of modesty.

One more thing we must remember is that in raising children, the most important thing is encouraging their enthusiasm. Children tend to become absorbed in things more easily than adults. To interrupt that enthusiasm because it is inconvenient for adults is like losing an extremely valuable jewel. For example, when the French entomologist Jean Henri Fabre (1823–1915) was engrossed in observing insects as a child, if his parents had said, "What are you doing? Get right back to your studies," then he might not have become the author of the landmark *Souvenirs entomologiques*. When children become deeply involved in something, they should be left alone, because there is no telling how that enthusiasm will eventually germinate. Perhaps even more important than some future concrete accomplishment is the development of the habit of total concentration. It will become the child's mainstay throughout life.

Devote yourself to one thing at a time, and you will feel fulfilled, find true meaning in life, and achieve something great.

One Million Recitations

I believe that life is *practice* and *discipline* from beginning to end. By practice and discipline I mean doing everything wholeheartedly—both physically and mentally—and repeatedly.

First, let us look at the matter of repetition. By repetition I do not mean simply doing the same thing again and again. What I mean bears similarity to the thread of a screw. When I look at a screw from the end, the thread appears as concentric circles, but seen from the side it spirals upward. As a result, as you turn the screw with a screwdriver, it bores its way in.

It is said that the way to master haiku is to compose a hundred a day. In baseball, they say that the only way for a reserve player to become a regular player is by the continued practice of swinging a bat a thousand times a day. Repetition deepens experience and wisdom, and is the fundamental way to build character.

It is the same way with work. No matter how monotonous the task, if you do it time and again wholeheartedly, each time you will make visible progress. At the very moment you awaken to that improvement, you will feel the will to work. At many places of work, the same task is repeated day in and day out. Some people grow weary of the monotony, losing interest in their jobs and the will to work. Whenever you feel that doing the same job every day is boring, I hope that you will recall the Japanese maxim for the tea ceremony, "One meeting, one chance." Become aware that the work before you is work that you will never encounter again in your entire life. It is true that, even if you do nothing today, tomorrow will come, but "tomorrow" is no more than a place on a calendar. If, on the other hand, you approach each day with the attitude that "today I will do today's work," then you will meet up with fresh work the following day. That day your day will be worthwhile.

By continuing in a single line of work, an engineer and a salesman will steadily develop their own essential competence, and will simultaneously cultivate pride and confidence in their work. Moreover, though they themselves may think of their jobs as just a means of earning a living and keeping food on the table, they are also building something very important—their characters.

Our age is in love with "instant" things, and we are becoming disinclined to devote time and steady labor to any single purpose. All the more because of this tendency, doing something over and over carefully and thoroughly will shine forth conspicuously.

The scholar of Japanese letters Hanawa Hokiichi (1746–1821) is credited with the immortal accomplishment of writing the *Gunsho Ruiju* (A Classified Collection of Japanese Classics) of over 1,500 volumes, which took him forty-one years to complete. Told by the blind acupuncturist Ametomi Sugaichi that to complete a major achievement during one's lifetime one needed the protection of the gods and buddhas, Hokiichi vowed to recite the Heart of Wisdom Sutra a million times. He made the vow at the age of twenty-seven, and from then until his death at the age of seventy-six he intoned the sutra a hundred times a day, not missing a single day, making a total of 1,935,000 repetitions.

A million times is easier said than done. The Heart of Wisdom Sutra is comparatively short, so a hundred recitations a day is possible, but a hundred every day without fail is a very strict practice and discipline. To intone the sutra 1,935,000 times is of great significance.

And now let us discuss the matter of doing something wholeheartedly. I have personally had the experience of copying the ten scrolls of the

Chinese translation of the Threefold Lotus Sutra, a scripture of well over eighty thousand characters. Secluding myself in the mountains of Hakone, I finished in fifty-five days. Before then I had without fail read and recited the scriptures each day, but as I copied them in my own hand, attending to the spirit of each character and each phrase, I experienced anew the merits of the sutra penetrating my soul. I will never forget that sensation. That is what it means to do something wholeheartedly both mentally and physically.

Recently, I hear, many Japanese college students do not take notes at lectures but merely buy copies of someone else's. I wonder whether they really learn much that way. I have serious reservations. Yoshida Shoin (1830–59), a philosopher and educator, said that half a reader's effort ought to be devoted to making notes of essential points, since reading alone is insufficient for a full understanding of something. Taking notes deepens one's understanding.

When Katsu Kaishu (1823–99) was twenty-six, his sword master told him that the future would not be an age of swords and that Japan needed Western-style coastal defenses. Katsu therefore resolved to study Dutch scientific works, then the only ones available in Japan. However, since his family was poor, he could not afford to buy a Dutch-Japanese dictionary. Instead, he borrowed one, made his own quill pen, and copied all fifty-eight volumes word for word. Moreover, he made two copies: one for himself and one to sell, and out of gratitude gave the proceeds to the lender of the dictionary. Above all, he felt that he would learn all the more by making two copies. It took Katsu a year and a half to complete the two copies, between caring for his invalid mother and looking after his younger sister. It can be imagined how great an impact that effort and tenacity had on the remainder of his life.

Even ordinary people can accomplish something of great value if they devote themselves to one particular thing wholeheartedly and repeatedly.

The Ordinary Way

When a baseball outfielder races for a batted ball and makes a successful diving catch, everyone applauds him for making a fine play. But in reality, a fine play is when the outfielder guesses where the batter is likely to hit the ball, goes to that spot, and makes the catch with ease. This is a simple strategy, but it is the ideal way to play baseball. We learn from this that what at first glance appears difficult can be surprisingly easy, and that it can be rather difficult to carry out calmly what appears quite commonplace.

This reminds me of an anecdote concerning the thirteenth-century swordsman Tsukahara Bokuden. One day, as five or six of his young followers were walking along a road, a horse tethered by the road suddenly kicked at one of them. When the young man nimbly dodged the blow, his companions were filled with admiration. They returned to their training hall and told their master what had happened. Tsukahara frowned and grumbled, "You have not practiced enough." The young followers protested and said, "If that is so, then please walk along that road and show us how you would deal with the horse." Tsukahara agreed. When they came to where the horse was tethered, Tsukahara walked briskly down the road on the side across from the horse.

He then admonished his disciples: "A horse kicks. You never know when it will kick. So whenever you go near a horse be sure not to get too close. Keeping your distance as you go by is how to be prepared. This is none other than the secret of swordsmanship." The baseball anecdote and Tsukahara's admonition hold true for anything in life.

The Japanese Buddhist term *shojin,* meaning assiduity, includes the meaning of doing ordinary things in ordinary ways. It is not the doing of something that is especially difficult or that borders on the impossible. Doing commonplace things, slowly but steadily, always with vigilance, always conscientiously—this is true assiduity.

There are all kinds of mottoes to encourage assiduity in the workplace, such as "Every employee is a salesman," "Devote yourself to cost-consciousness," and "A debt of long standing is comparable to a tenfold decrease in sales." Each is important, but if one becomes overly inclined

toward developing competent people, one will
end up merely developing skills. Someone once
said, "It is enough for a man to read books, keep
company with friends, and polish his sword." If
we adapt this recommendation for businessmen,
it might be, "Continually expand your informa-
tion network," and "Cultivate your job skills."
These maxims alone, however, seem a bit bleak.
Why not go one step further? "Constantly delve
into yourself," "Cultivate your ability to consider
others," and "Polish the sword that cuts off
worldly desires."

With capable employees a company's short-
term performance is sure to improve. But it is the
nurturing of a solid spiritual framework among
its employees that will guarantee a company a
century of prosperity. It seems to me that good
fortune over the long run depends on quite ordinary actions, such as greeting others first, keeping
promises, and not complaining or making ex-
cuses. If one can unflaggingly do commonplace
things every day, that is all that is necessary.
More than being merely sufficient, it may even be
called the secret of assiduity.

Before attaining enlightenment, the Buddha for
six years practiced continual austerities at the risk
of his life, but finally realized that this was not
the way to truth. After bathing in a river, he ate
the milk gruel a village maiden offered him. Not
bathing in rivers and not eating nutritious foods
had been part of his austerities. Renouncing as-
ceticism and returning to the life of an ordinary

person, he fell once again into contemplation and ultimately attained enlightenment. The essence of his teachings from then on was that by living in truth and doing the right thing, all people will find happiness, and the whole world will be at peace.

Many people want to work in their own way, but work means serving someone wholeheartedly. When you forget the feeling of being of service, what you do becomes mere labor and the joy disappears. An important point concerning work has been made by the late Etai Yamada, the head of the Tendai sect of Japanese Buddhism and chief priest of its head temple, Enryaku-ji, on Mount Hiei. He said, "The two characters *shi* and *goto* [compounded as the Japanese word for 'work'] have the following meaning: *shi* means 'take service under' and *goto* means 'thing.' Therefore 'work' means the hardships you endure and the pleasure you take in listening to the ideas of your employer, superiors, colleagues, and others as you carry out your duties."

Another important element of assiduity is doing one's best.

Hibiya Park in central Tokyo is Japan's first Western-style park. It was designed by Seiroku Honda (1866–1952), Japan's first doctor of forestry. Honda enrolled in the school that later became the agriculture department of the University of Tokyo, but because he was largely self-taught, he had considerable difficulty with the subjects he had not studied. He fared worst in geometry, and in the first term he conspicuously failed it. To atone to his parents, he made up his mind to throw himself down a well, but was unable to go through with it. Though he was not to die, Honda determined to study as if he had. He got hold of a collection of one thousand geometry problems and determined to solve them one by one. Once he had started, he gradually became interested and began to understand them. He completed all one thousand. The next term he made perfect scores on the examinations and was so good at the subject that the professor told him, "You have a real genius for geometry, so you needn't attend my lectures anymore." This is an example of the rewards of assiduity. Doing one's very best is implicitly and explicitly accompanied by this sort of reward.

Over and above the eventual rewards of assiduity, there is a spiritual merit that one can savor right on the spot. That is the sense of satisfaction, the feeling of fulfillment, you feel when you can say, "I've done my best." Once you relish that deep satisfaction, you will want to experience it once more, and from then on, whether you are doing the same thing or something else, you will always do your best. When this happens, your work will become interesting and your life will take on greater value. You will feel an irresistible enjoyment in everything. There is no greater merit than this.

Assiduity does not mean trying to do something espe-

*cially difficult, but working at ordinary things stead-
ily, diligently, and to the best of one's ability.*

Cold Birds and Barrels of Oil

Effort and assiduity are the most fundamental
ways to improve ourselves. The significance of
these basic virtues is the same in study, work,
management, and life in general, but because
they are so basic, we on occasion neglect them. In
the same way, despite the fact that air and water
are absolutely vital for our existence, people do
not seem to notice them.

Although we realize that we cannot accomplish
anything by working halfheartedly, we often take
the easy way out, thinking that it does not matter
whether we apply ourselves today or tomorrow
or neglect our work. The Buddha admonishes
us to shun this attitude by way of the parable
of a mythical bird in the Himalayas. The Hima-
layan nights are extremely cold, and the female
of the species seems to cry all night long, "I'm
dying of cold. I'm dying of cold." The male
seems to cry through the night, "Build a nest at
dawn. Build a nest at dawn." With no nest to
keep them warm, the night is unbearably cold,
and they wait for dawn to build a nest for shelter.
However, when morning comes and the sun
shines, they are carefree in the warmth of its rays.
They forget about building a nest and pass the
day leisurely. Predictably, when night falls, they

suffer from the extreme cold and take up their cries again. They continue this until the end of their lives.

We should not laugh at their folly. There are many people who neglect to build "a nest for the spirit" in which they can always be at ease, no matter how the world around them changes. Engrossed in what is right in front of them, they tell themselves, "I'll get around to it sometime soon. Sometime before long." They completely neglect to make consistent efforts toward that end. When things get tough, they become a bit more serious, but when things lighten up, they become neglectful again. They never build a nest that would give them peace of mind. Any nest they do manage to build is the kind that blows away in the first strong wind or leaves them soaked in the first rain. This is the weakness of not being consistent. If only they were thorough, that nest would be a secure fortress lasting their whole lives. But they are unable to take that one step forward.

There was once a Standard Oil Company employee named John D. Archbold (1848–1916), whose colleagues never called him by his real name. Instead they always called him "Four dollars a barrel." The reason was that when he traveled and registered at a hotel, he would always write under his name "Four dollars a barrel, Standard Oil." He did the same when signing letters and receipts. When John D. Rockefeller, the president of Standard Oil, heard about this unusual employee, he was so impressed that he invited him to dinner. Archbold came to enjoy Rockefeller's confidence, and many years later he became the company's second president. That he came to be recognized and relied on by Rockefeller was neither chance nor mere good fortune. It resulted, rather, from his being so thorough in his daily efforts that he earned a nickname for it. There are many such success stories in America, but this one has a particularly valuable moral, that thoroughness creates the real thing.

Tettei, the Japanese word for thoroughness, is originally a Buddhist term. The Bodhisattva Universal Virtue appears in the Lotus Sutra as a symbol of the preeminence of thoroughgoing practice. He is always mounted on a white elephant, because an elephant crossing a river always steps firmly. Universal Virtue would have us understand that this kind of steadiness is important in carrying out any action.

During the early eighteenth century in Japan, there was an eminent mathematician named Noda Bunzo. Hearing of his abilities, Yoshimune, the eighth Tokugawa shogun, consulted Ooka Tadasuke, the commissioner of Edo, about giving Noda some appointment. Ooka summoned Noda and asked him, "I hear that you are quite learned in calculations, so tell me, what is one hundred divided by two?" From his bosom Noda took out his abacus, did the calculation, and replied, "One hundred divided by two is fifty, sir." Being careful enough to use his abacus even for a simple computation he could have done in his head is a fine example of thoroughness.

How can we become thorough? By *always seeking and practicing.* "Always" means never forgetting to do something. "Seeking" means a desire for self-improvement in the search for religious truth. And "practicing" means the actual translation of that desire into action. Doing these three things unceasingly is the secret of acquiring thoroughness. If any one of the three is neglected, thoroughness goes out the window. In short, thoroughness means not allowing oneself to be distracted, but pushing on without a pause. That is the secret of success.

With the spirit of thoroughness, that is, always seeking and practicing, you are bound to succeed.

BE TRUE TO YOURSELF

A Buddha's Countenance
Shines Through

The face is a fascinating part of the body. Most
people, when they are born and when they die,
have a serene, buddhalike expression. The problem is the interval between these two events.
There are great differences among people. The
faces of those who have done many good deeds
look cheerful and refreshing; the faces of those
who have done one bad deed after another are
darkened by some sort of shadow.

One of the many reasons I enjoy watching tele-
vision is that I can see so many different faces; it
is as if the people were standing right in front of
me. I sense that a scholar looks like a scholar, a
teacher like a teacher, a doctor like a doctor. If the
doctor is a pediatrician, it is obvious at a glance.
The face is always gentle and kind. Long years of
medical practice have given that face its special
features.

In the world of sumo wrestling, most young
men join a training organization when they are

fifteen or sixteen, and live with and train under a master. The trainees seem to develop a certain resemblance to their master. In the nineteenth and early twentieth centuries, young maidservants employed in wealthy households came to resemble the lady of the house after living so many years with her.

The attractiveness of someone's face is not determined by their features but by their heart, their character, and their experience. Everyone has seen that even a pedigreed dog can look stupid, and that a well-trained sheep dog may look clever. This is even truer of people. A well-known episode in the life of Abraham Lincoln illustrates his awareness of how a face reflects character. When Lincoln became president a friend proposed a middle-aged acquaintance for a post in the government, and Lincoln agreed to interview him. After the interview Lincoln told his friend he would not be able to employ the man. When asked why, Lincoln replied that he had been put off by the man's looks. When asked how even a president could judge someone by his looks, Lincoln replied that a man who has reached the age of forty is responsible for his looks. A Japanese master of aphorisms, Soichi Oya (1900–1979), wrote in much the same vein, "A man's face is his résumé."

Moreover, I believe that the face is the window of the soul. My respected mentor, the former chief priest of the temple Kiyomizu-dera in Kyoto, Rev. Ryokei Onishi (1875–1983), wrote in

Zazen Wasan Kowa (Discourses on the Hymns in Praise of Zazen) that no one looks like an aristocrat or *daimyo* (feudal baron) at birth. Babies tend to look alike. But a boy brought up as an aristocrat or *daimyo* acquires something of a natural dignity, whatever his features. He went on:

> So someone like me does not count for anything. I am poor, so sometimes I eat and sometimes I do not. I am always thinking about what the day will bring, so my face has come to look this way. Whether a man has really eaten or not, if he always tries to look like he has, keeps his dignity, and wears an expression like the richest man in town, it will leave permanent traces in his face. And if a man thinks he is essentially a buddha, he will come to look like one.

Buddhist scriptures offer another example. There was once a somewhat dimwitted young man named Chulapanthaka who, with his more intelligent brother, went to the Jetavana Monastery to join the Buddhist Order. During his training, however, he could not memorize even a single verse of a sutra and was driven out by the older followers of the Buddha. As he stood sobbing at the gate, the Buddha appeared and led him back inside, handed him a broom, and told him to recite over and over as he swept, "Sweep away the dust," and "Take away the dirt." Day after day as he swept the rooms clean, Chulapanthaka tried his best to recite these phrases, but if he remembered "Sweep away the dust," he would forget "Take away the dirt." As months passed, however, he succeeded in remembering both phrases, and after doing that for several months eventually attained enlightenment. One day his brother, whom he had not seen for a long time, came to the monastery to visit him and saw a new light in Chulapanthaka's eyes and radiance in his face. Struck by these facial changes, the elder brother incredulously exclaimed that Chulapanthaka had attained enlightenment. Among the Buddha's followers were many great figures like Shariputra and Maudgalyayana, but nothing they did inspires us with as much courage as Chulapanthaka's transformation.

Since we are all the Buddha's children, we should try not to think ignoble, improper, scheming thoughts, but regularly recall that we are in essence buddhas, and engrave that thought on our hearts. In our daily lives we should determine to behave like children of the Buddha. If we do that, our faces will take on a look of nobility, others will like and respect us, and we will get along well with them.

The face is the window of the soul. Acquisitive or short-tempered though we may be, we will unknowingly take on a look of amiability if we make a habit of giving alms and greeting others with a smile.

The Key to a Radiant Smile

Young people today want to be better understood. Of course, this feeling is not limited to the young; the same strong desire is found in the heart of almost every human being. And yet despite that heartfelt wish, young people are unwilling to disclose their true selves. Herein lies a great contradiction. Because they are not honest with themselves, they are not understood, and their own radiance does not shine forth.

People often wonder why I am always smiling, and they ask me, "Is there some secret to it?" I usually reply, "No, there's no secret. It's just that I always try to be myself. That's probably the reason why I always smile."

People often try to make themselves look better than they really are, and by doing so they often make it hard on themselves. It is as if they are always standing on tiptoe. Though it is more than enough just to plant both feet firmly on the ground, if one stretches and stands on the toes, the feet will start to hurt, one totters, and one has to endure it all, so naturally it becomes a torment. Of course, there are occasions when one needs to look one's best. However, the effort of always trying to overreach oneself makes one feel awkward and irritable. When one feels this way, simply telling oneself, "I am what I am," and just being oneself produces relaxation and ease.

Thanks to this practice, I have been able to

spend my days with this sort of serenity. As I look back, I see that I have always been myself and showed my feelings. To be sure, I have also run into difficulties. There were some tough times, like the seven years I was constantly pawning my formal kimono, redeeming it only to pawn it again. Yet even then I was wearing a smile, and for as long as I can remember, people have been commenting about this habit. When I reflect on why I have been able to let people see just who I am, I can only conclude that it has been because I believe that if only I entrust myself to the Buddha, everything will turn out all right.

The strain of overreaching oneself not only is psychological, but also has economic manifestations in daily life. For example, it would seem that many Japanese these days feel no great hesitation about borrowing money. On the contrary, to investors it appears entirely reasonable to borrow capital at low interest to buy land or shares or make other investments. Even individuals, instead of paying off the home loans they already have, borrow more money, often through the use of credit cards, to buy cars or furniture or to pay for travel.

Is there not a pitfall in feeling that borrowing money is a natural, even positive, sort of behavior? Yukichi Fukuzawa (1835–1901) writes in his *Fukuo Jiden* (The Autobiography of Fukuzawa Yukichi), "On the whole, aside from assassination, there is nothing in this world as frightening to me as borrowing money." According to

Fukuzawa's rationale, if one borrows money, it is only right to return it, so if it is an amount one can return anyway, one should make up one's mind not to borrow, but to save until one has the sum in hand. Fukuzawa writes that he never borrowed money, even small amounts. He goes on to say, "In short, I am extremely timid when it comes to going into debt; I have not the least bit of courage. To have borrowed money and then have to worry about not being able to repay it on demand seems to me like being pursued by someone with a drawn sword." If people today were as fearful of debt as Fukuzawa, there would certainly be no suffering from onerous repayment of bank loans or overused credit cards.

In Japan there is a saying, "One cannot live seventy days, but one can live seventy years." If one makes a serious mistake on the job, risks bankruptcy, or is burdened by a loan that is unpayable, one may feel unable to go on living. But the feeling lasts at most seventy days, and before one knows it, one somehow recovers. Before long, another crisis arises, and though one once again sinks into despair, it too eventually passes. Before one notices it, one has attained the age of seventy. Life goes on.

I believe that one feeling in particular is crucial for going through life easily. This is the feeling that if one lives with the spirit of the Buddha, there can be no greater happiness. The ultimate will of the Buddha is the desire for every person, every being, just to be true to themselves. A line from the Noh chant *Basho* expresses it in this way:

> As in the parable of the herbs,
> Even grass, trees, and earth,
> Sentient and nonsentient—
> Every one of these is of
> The "reality of all existence."
> The tempest at the summit
> And the sound of water in the valley
> Do the Buddha's work.

The terminology here may be slightly unfamiliar, so allow me to explain. "The Parable of the Herbs" is the title of chapter 5 of the Lotus Sutra. "Sentient" refers to things that have a soul, and "nonsentient" refers to things that are not believed to have a soul. "The reality of all existence" means the true nature of all things, exactly as they are. In other words, the sounds of both the tempest on the mountaintop and the water of the stream flowing through the valley express the spirit of the Buddha. Because of the universal presence of the buddha-nature, insentient things like grass, trees, and earth, as well as sentient beings, can attain buddhahood. The Buddha's spirit exists in grass and trees, mountains and rivers, all things in the world harmonizing just as they are.

Let us fling away this desire to make ourselves seem better than we really are, and let us manifest the buddha-nature by just being the way we are and by living in accordance with our true nature. We must simply recall that human beings do not live in the buddha-nature all alone. Thus, we hope that those around us will come to live in the same way, and we should begin to work toward that end. This is one respect, in contrast to the tempest on the mountaintop and the stream in the valley, in which we can express the Buddha's spirit.

I have always made an effort to live in the spirit of the Buddha. I believe that is why I am always at ease and why I am always smiling.

Opening yourself to others just as you are is the most carefree way to live.

Knowing Your Role

It seems as if each and every human being has a unique way of living, yet in another way everyone seems very much the same. For example, while desiring to place importance on their own feelings and individuality, the majority of Japanese feel that they are alike in sharing a middle-class lifestyle. When it comes to the essential quality of all phenomena, we must remember that everything—not only human beings, but also grass and trees—consists of a single, all-pervading element.

However, the manner in which this element is manifested varies. No two people are exactly alike. By becoming aware of these differences, we can know what makes each person's way of life unique. On the plains and in the mountains, the cedar forests are a deep green. In autumn the oaks, maples, and sumacs tint the mountains yellow and red. The eulalia heads flow in silver waves. The bellflowers put forth their lovely violet blossoms. And the bases of large trees are covered with blankets of incomparably beautiful moss. This is what in Buddhism we call *jinen honi,* the spontaneous working of the universal law, and because of it the beauty of nature increases in radiance. Each thing has its own individual beauty, and all things interact harmoniously. How would it be if each flower and plant were to insist on equality in size, color, and character? Our world would become characterless, and furthermore, would gradually die. For example, if all the plants were to soar toward the sky and become evergreens, the sunlight could not penetrate to the undergrowth, the nutrients in the soil would be depleted, and all the trees and plants would die. That is why there is such a complex, diversified distribution of plants in nature today.

Perhaps human beings have forgotten that they are all essentially equal and that, at the same time, everyone has their own individuality. I wonder if we press for equality in name only and whether everyone has the unnatural desire to become a large evergreen.

There is a Japanese proverb about a crow that tries to imitate a cormorant. In the same way, when one loses sight of one's own uniqueness, everything gets turned around. On the other hand, some people become negligent in the belief that they are worthless. This, too, is shirking responsibility.

Each human being is blessed by the gods and buddhas with a role that only he or she can carry out. It is a pleasure to watch a carpenter plane lumber or a gardener prune trees. Each time I see such people at work, I am impressed with their skill, and I feel refreshed. This is the beauty of being oneself. In this big, wide world there is a place that only you can fill. By doing your best, you live in a way that is worthy of the role you are entrusted with, and fill the place that only you can fill. You are neither pressured nor constrained by anyone else. As an old saying goes, when one concentrates on one's work and does one's best, "Food will be on the table, and the sun will rise." If one is satisfied with what follows, one gains peace of mind.

We are constantly measuring ourselves against expectations others have of us. Men try to be manly, women womanly; teachers try to be good teachers, and students good students. On the job, some people try to be, for instance, good bank clerks or good trading-company employees. Recently it seems that fewer and fewer people cling to these admittedly ambiguous standards and that more and more people have come to believe that the best way to live is to do as you wish. Their reaction against professional standards may be due to their feeling constrained by the requirement that they fit into one single mold, but this seems to me a grand illusion. It might seem that one can live as one likes if one is free from having to measure up to expectations, but this does not mean that there is any great goal to be achieved this way. Rather, is it not often the case that one is simply swayed by the small, insignificant self? Instead of giving way to self-indulgence, if one devotes oneself to improving one's abilities, one will surely be able to realize one's potential. In the process of realizing your potential, your individuality grows beyond the bounds of imagination. On the job or among neighbors, those who devote themselves fully to allotted tasks are entrusted with ever-expanding responsibilities.

Some people will not be ignored. They cannot help acquiring popularity, position, and reputation. Moreover, they have a good moral influence on the people around them. Shigesaburo Maeo (1905–81), who was a speaker of Japan's House of Representatives, wrote about Sada Iwamoto, his respected teacher at the prestigious First Higher School. Iwamoto taught philosophy and German. In class he would loudly and vigorously scold students, and he was so strict in grading examinations that of a class of forty students, almost half would fail. Despite this, after his death his admiring students raised a monument to him at the temple Soji-ji in Yokohama. In the passage where he tells of this, Maeo writes, "And now fifty years later I have completely forgotten my German, and I remember nothing of the outline of philosophy that I studied except the opening lines. But I acquired a devotion to scholarship, and it is impossible for me to measure just how well that has served me over the years."

I am not alone in feeling that Iwamoto was an excellent teacher.

From a different perspective, Japanese people certainly ought to be acutely conscious of just how important it is for all things to remain true to themselves. With pollution-related diseases, the worsening of the quality of our air and water, and the degradation of our land, forests, and seas, we have become painfully aware that our very existence as human beings is threatened when things stop conforming to the laws of the universe. In our hearts we entertain fears of what it would be like for humanity to lose its humanness.

Being true to oneself is not a matter of coercion, but is rather a spontaneous way of living that proceeds from knowing the laws of the universe.

Be aware that you are assigned a role that only you can play, and you will be true to yourself.

Self-Esteem

The word *conceit* is never used in a positive sense. It means excessive pride in one's abilities. Benjamin Franklin, a member of the committee that drafted the American Declaration of Independence, once said something to the effect that no matter how conceited one might be, the conceit

of others gets on one's nerves. Since everyone
shares that attitude, the word has negative conno-
tations.

Probably everyone feels superior to others in
some way. I have a certain amount of conceit myself. But I believe that making it a source of energy for cheerful living is a rather clever way to
live. Being conceited or vain means being attached to oneself, affirming oneself, and loving
oneself. Therefore, although a puffed-up person
may appear foolish, he or she will be able to go
through life cheerfully, with a sense of well-being
and a positive attitude. Moreover, though at first
such an attitude may border on overconfidence,
before long one may actually develop genuine
self-confidence. I have seen many cases where
this has been true. This approach to life not only
makes one happy, but also produces radiance
and benefits society.

The exact opposite of this is the inferiority complex. Because one depreciates oneself in every
conceivable way, one's life is unhappy. Those
nearby feel that one is dreary and disagreeable.
Since others do not respond favorably and turn
their backs, one's sense of inferiority ends up
growing more and more acute. When we investi-
gate the origin of this sense of inferiority, we find
that it springs from a minor sense of inadequacy.
If we feel that we have one or two minor flaws—
something to do with personal appearance, figure, health, intelligence, ability, athletic prowess,
family, or academic background—that sense of

inadequacy can harm our whole attitude. We come to feel completely worthless and end up making ourselves unhappy, with no help from others.

By way of clarification, a sense of inferiority is different from a temporary feeling of self-disgust. When we fail in some way or some meanness arises within us, we feel wretched. But this kind of momentary aversion to oneself is the action of a healthy spirit, the generative power that helps a person become a better human being. An inferiority complex, however, serves only to make one obsequious and cave in.

One of the first astronauts said that our planet looked blue from above. If he had been able to see the over four billion human beings that live on this blue planet, he would surely have seen each one as a similar dot on the face of the earth. Without having to fly as high as a spacecraft, we can climb to the top of a mountain or tall building and see how humans appear as mere dots on the ground below. From that height we cannot distinguish men from women, the wise from the foolish, or the intrepid from the fainthearted. If we place ourselves in their midst we realize that we, too, are just like everyone else. From this more encompassing point of view, we begin to feel that it is useless to fret over trifles, and we begin to be impressed at how energetically everyone is working to get along in life.

Through its subtle workings, nature produces a great variety of human beings. It is because there are so many different people that our world is brought into equilibrium and is so full of interest. How would it be if everyone were made from the same mold with identical facial features, physiques, and capabilities? Admittedly, there might no longer be such a thing as an inferiority complex, but it would be just as well for the human race to be replaced by robots.

Superficially, everyone seems to have unique elements of beauty and ugliness, wisdom and folly, strength and weakness. But deep inside, everyone has the same buddha-nature. One grain of sand, one blade of grass, one single human being: the existence of each of these things has a cause and serves a need. This is a truth beyond refutation. If one gives some thought to this truth, one becomes keenly aware that there is a reason for living, and that one's existence has dignity.

We are apt to be caught up in comparing ourselves with others and in competing with them. Because of that, we become mean-spirited, always conscious that others are judging us. We lose sight of the truth that the gods and buddhas provide us with suitable roles. When we go further awry, we begin to lose confidence and feel inferior.

There is absolutely no one on earth who does not have some special talent and some way of being of service to the world. Discovering what that talent or way of being is and prizing it is extremely important, not only for ourselves, but also for the world at large.

Wisdom is turning conceit that we cannot avoid into a strength.

Yielding Will Teach You Magnanimity

In our everyday lives we usually give thought to work, the way we live, our families, and a variety of other affairs. Something is always coming up that requires our attention, and we might go so far as to say that we are constantly pursued by such things. When we are enmeshed in pressing matters and are occupied only with what happens around us, however, our outlook cannot but become narrower. *My* desires, *my* advantage, *my* feelings, and *my* activities—no matter what we do, we cannot escape from the self, and our hearts become filled with "me." In human relationships, if everyone asserts this self unhindered, it clashes with others' selves, and there is no end of trouble.

The secret of making a clean sweep of all such troubles is the spirit of humility. To humble oneself means becoming selfless and open-minded. This definition of humility is not regularly found in dictionaries, and it is based on respect for other people.

According to Lao-tsu,

> The highest good is like water.
> Water gives life to the ten thousand things
> And does not strive.

It flows in places people avoid
And so is like the Way.

Water is a precious thing that gives moisture to all living things, sustaining grasses, trees, and crops. It never flows against other things, but instead flows into places that most people avoid and stays there in peace. Herein lies the modest spirit. Learning humility means committing oneself to getting along with all people and things, first by seeking out the good in others and greatly valuing it. People who do this are modest.

Stubborn as human beings may seem on the surface, deep inside we nurture tender hearts. If we stubbornly assert ourselves, other people will also grow obstinate. Conversely, if we are willing to take one big step backward and give way, other people will naturally soften. If anything, asserting ourselves is the way of our world, and retreating makes us feel as if we are losing, so it is quite difficult to take that first small step. This is particularly true among young people, because they place such great emphasis on self-assertion. Nevertheless, unless someone is willing to discard the small self in order to attain a greater harmony, the clash of self with self will continue incessantly. Magnanimous people will, at the point of conflict, take a step backward and accept what others have to say. By doing so, they remove all resistance, and nothing remains for the others to collide with.

Those who are capable of great accomplishments always realize the truth that sometimes the best way to win is to lose. The sixteenth-century warlord Toyotomi Hideyoshi (at one time lord of Chikuzen) was a good example of this. When his lord, Oda Nobunaga, was struck down in the Honno-ji Incident in 1582, Hideyoshi immediately withdrew his troops from the siege of Takamatsu Castle in Bitchu province and crushed Akechi Mitsuhide on the outskirts of Kyoto. Following these events, the various generals loyal to Oda gathered at the castle in Nobunaga's home province. At the evening banquet Shibata Katsuie, the general and governor of Echizen, became drunk and lay down. He said to Hideyoshi, "It seems quite strange when one thinks about the past. When you were just an underling you used to massage my legs and hips, and now you have suddenly risen to the status of lord like me. I'm tired and would like someone to rub the small of my back, but I surely couldn't ask you to do that." The various commanders in the room fell silent, and Sakuma Morimasa, as if to mediate between the two, whispered to Hideyoshi, "If the past cannot be forgotten, why not accede to his request?" Hideyoshi looked down for a moment and finally replied, "If I may be of service." He edged over to Katsuie, massaged his back very carefully, and quietly returned to his seat. At this point Sakuma suddenly turned irritable and said, "Lord of Chikuzen, for a commissioner at the western headquarters, you have behaved disgracefully. Consider the rank conferred on you by our late lord. If it is to be this way, I cannot sit idly by. Come now, I will challenge you." Saying this, he abruptly stood up. Hideyoshi, however, merely responded with a smile. "What you have said is quite true, but this is a time of crisis. If those of the inner circle begin to bicker, the enemy will surely take advantage of it. Rubbing Lord Shibata's back is only a way of being of service to our late lord." Sakuma could do nothing but fall silent. Later it came to light that, out of fear that the realm was falling under Hideyoshi's control, Shibata and Sakuma had conspired to humiliate him, provoke him to a duel, and kill him. In the end Hideyoshi, by yielding amicably, became ruler of the nation.

Many who hear that story may think that in Japan in feudal times it was either kill or be killed. Nowadays, if you always yield, you will come out a loser. However, though times have changed, the same reasoning holds true. Though we occasionally endure loss, it is only a loss in the short run. When seen from a long-term perspective, something fortunate may result from a loss, and everything balances out in the end. Even if we seem to be consistently taking losses, it means that we are constantly serving others, and as a consequence, as our good reputation grows, others will gather around.

In associating with your friends, if you never concede in anything, you will drift apart from each other. In business, if we are never willing to make a concession at any stage of a negotiation, we will never achieve great things. When it appears that the other side has no intention of yielding, we should make a virtue of necessity by giving way. If we do this, the other side will never forget the favor. Eventually it may result in a large order or a long-term business relationship; in other words, we may sow a loss and reap a gain.

Ordinarily, yielding is accompanied by some form of self-sacrifice, either material or spiritual. However, this kind of sacrifice, on a higher level, provides something of inestimable value.

By yielding with a smile and accepting a loss willingly, you achieve spiritual growth.

There Is Freedom in Staying on the Path

We live our lives under a number of restraints. But if we shift our perspective a little, we can see that what appear to be restrictions on our freedom actually provide us with support.

One of humanity's ultimate desires is probably the desire for complete freedom. Since time immemorial, human beings have always sought to be free—free from the menaces of nature, free from hunger, free from disease, and free from political oppression. However, it does not seem that society can break all of these restrictions. As soon as one is eliminated, a new one appears in its place. For example, the car and the airplane were invented out of a desire to travel freely and quickly over long distances, but they have brought us new hindrances in the forms of air pollution, noise, and accidents. Does this mean that complete freedom is unattainable? Not necessarily.

In addition to the freedoms guaranteed by our civil rights laws, we have one more, very special freedom. That is the freedom of the soul, something inherent in each of us. We can exercise this freedom when we take a walk. When we walk on the sidewalk we can relax and walk leisurely. However, if we step off the sidewalk and into the road, we do not have a moment free of anxiety. In other words, accepting the restrictions of the sidewalk means freedom, and we can walk there with ease. It may help to remember that, even in the most fundamental, physical sense, we cannot be completely freed of bonds. It is because of the earth's gravity that we can stand or sit. Were it not for gravitational pull, we would not be able to walk with our feet on the ground. We would be like toy balloons floating here and there, unable to go in the direction of our choice. That would be just the opposite of freedom.

Buddhism teaches *muso* (formlessness) and *musa* (inaction). Though all things have form, one should not become caught up in mere appearances. We have a stomach and intestines—things that have form—and when they function correctly, we forget that they exist. This is "formlessness." As we walk we put out one leg, then the other, and we do not consciously consider that we are following certain rules. When the left leg goes forward, the right arm swings forward. When the right leg moves forward, the left arm does, too. We are unconscious of it all. This is what is meant by "inaction." In this way our entire daily life is *muso* and *musa,* and we behave ourselves without thinking, so we do not stray from the path. If this can be attained, then life becomes absolutely free, with no hardship or suffering.

The Buddhist Sanskrit term *sila* (precept) originally meant "good living habits." Its meaning is closer to "practical theory" than to "rules." In baseball, rugby, and other sports there is a theoretically "proper" way to catch, throw, run, and kick. Those who ignore it and do things their own way often make mistakes. Some athletes seem to come to a dead end in their careers and make no further progress. It is through steady practice in accordance with theory that one surpasses the mean and becomes an expert, a "person of inaction" who can unconsciously cope with even unforeseen situations.

It is the same in life. We are taught rules, that is, practical theory of behavior. Following the path of right living, a path laid out over generations, is the basis for becoming a free person. Buddhism teaches the *vinaya,* or rules. Rules, too, are based on experience. In both the home and society at large, rules or laws are established when someone behaves in a way that is seen as disruptive to overall order, and the family or community determines to stop it from occurring again.

In sports, those who ignore the relevant theory will simply not be able to improve, but if they ignore the rules, there will be no game. Therefore, one is penalized for breaking a rule. So to do well in a sport, one obeys the rules, hones one's skills, and tries to figure out how to defeat the opponent. When players do this, the sport becomes an activity with infinite depth.

In society there are cases of businesses prospering outside the law; but without proper effort, ingenuity, and appropriate research, in due course such enterprises will, without exception, be assessed heavy penalties. On the contrary, by obeying the law and diligently endeavoring to overcome shortcomings one at a time, a business will naturally grow.

The Buddha said, "The one who can overcome the self is the greatest of all conquerors." Georges Clemenceau (1841–1929), the French premier during the last years of World War I, was a daring, determined statesman known as "the Tiger." It is said that Clemenceau's strength of will facilitated the Allied victory after a series of bitter battles. However, this is not the victory to which I call attention. Clemenceau was a great aficionado of cigars. He apparently smoked them all day, and his physician became worried and warned him to limit himself to six a day. Clemenceau is reported to have responded, "Well, if I am to limit myself to a mere six, I might as well swear off them entirely." Before long, however, a box of cigars reappeared on the premier's desk and was always open. Someone said to him, "I thought Your Excellency had given up smoking." Clemenceau replied, "The joy of victory is greatest after a hard battle. With these cigars I love so much right before my eyes, I am fighting a hard battle." In the last year of the war, Clemenceau was eventually able to gain mastery over himself.

When one seeks to live up to a certain decision, one's worst enemy is oneself. Since people nowadays are not taught the joy of "conquering the self," they see various rules only as restrictions on their freedom. Staying on the path may at first give one a feeling of restriction. However, by following the path, one realizes that that feeling of restraint is actually a springboard to betterment and self-renewal. And if one continues to persevere tenaciously, that feeling of restriction will vanish like clouds and mist. One will not be bound by anything but instead will have a carefree frame of mind. It is in precisely this attitude that true freedom exists.

This is not a special path. Anyone—right this very moment—can set forth on it.

Following the right path gives you peace and true freedom.

THE TWO FUNCTIONS OF A CELL

The Pleasure of Doing a Good Deed

It is said that there are about 500 million starving people in our world. Wars have deprived many people of their homes and driven them off their land. Japan is now fortunate to be free of famine and war, but we should not rest comfortably just because we happen to be so blessed.

Shimazu Nariakira, the nineteenth-century lord of the Satsuma domain (now Kagoshima Prefecture), was renowned for his great insight and judgment. He claimed that it takes at least ten years to see whether an enterprise will aquire a solid foundation. The Japanese Committee of the World Conference on Religion and Peace (WCRP/Japan) has continued its permanent Donate One Meal Campaign for more than fifteen years. It was originally proposed by Rev. Yasusaburo Tazawa, the leader of Shoroku Shinto Yamatoyama (a new Shinto organization). It encourages people to fast one or two days a month to share in a small way the suffering of those who starve. The money that would otherwise have been spent on all of these meals is contributed to the Fund for Peace and Development of WCRP/Japan, which provides food to starving people in developing nations. The Donate One Meal Campaign has won acceptance among religionists not only in Japan but around the world. It is a way in which anyone, anywhere, at any time, can help others. I am convinced that this is why it has gained such wide approval.

There are people who think that helping those in distress is something special, but I believe that it is a matter of course. As I have pointed out repeatedly, nothing in the world exists entirely of its own accord; all things are interrelated and mutually sustaining. If you think about the way we are all interconnected like the meshes of a net, you will see that helping others is also a way of helping yourself. Goethe said something to the effect that within the virtuous human soul dwells the noble sentiment that it is unforgivable for one person alone to be fortunate. It follows that one must seek one's own fortune in the good fortune of others.

Everyone wishes, deep in their heart, for everyone around them to achieve happiness. So we must do all we can to help others. Unfortunately, there is also a troublesome thing in the human heart known as self-interest—a nagging tendency to think first of what we might do to make our own lives easier regardless of the effect on others. Thinking this way, we come to feel that helping others is merely an irksome chore. However, when we look closely at the real situation and set aside this attitude for a moment, we surely comprehend that mutual support is part of human nature.

This is as clear as day, even in the way our bodies work. The human body is said to be composed of about 60 trillion cells. Physiologists have ascertained that every cell has two distinct functions. One is to take nutrients from the blood, assimilate them, and excrete the waste; in other words, to tend to the business of the cell. What I want to draw attention to is the second function, which is to assist the functions of the other cells; for example, supplying hormones to other cells and providing them with enzymes. Hence the 60 trillion cells that make up the body both continue their own lives and, by assisting the functioning of other cells, fulfill responsibilities as members of a larger community. They in no way compete with one another. In balancing give and take, they coexist and coprosper. Although the interdependency of cells in the human body is a neat system, fundamental human relationships are characterized by a jarring awkwardness, attributable to what we call self-centeredness. How might this imperfection be remedied? All would go well, of course, if we would each cast aside our self-centered thinking. But such thinking has been part of human nature for thousands of years, and is unlikely to be overcome at a single stroke.

There is, however, one infallible remedy for it:

service to others. Any form of service will do. Small kindnesses are enough. In the very beginning, performing these might seem a little bothersome, but if you summon up the courage, they are done easily enough. After doing a small kindness, one is filled with an indescribable joy. One's heart feels at ease, because such a deed accords with the law of nature. It is natural, like a train traveling smoothly on two rails. A poem by the thirteenth-century Zen master Dogen says it this way:

The ferryman takes others one by one
To the Other Shore without alighting himself.

As long as others suffer and are in need, we devote ourselves to helping them reach, before we do, the other shore of enlightenment. In thus forgetting the self, we follow the bodhisattva way.

The late Dr. Kiyoshi Oka, in his *Shunsho Juwa* (Ten Tales of a Spring Evening), makes the following point:

People of a slightly earlier time knew much better than we do the special quality of good deeds, and to make these easier there were ways to communicate that quality in the home. It was one of the values of this nation that if one did good deeds, all would go well, so there was no philosophy, or need of any. If in this way people constantly do good, their feelings gradually become nobler. As a result, they come to understand well the feelings of others and therefore cannot help doing good deeds all the more.

Besides savoring these words, it is important to see the cycle that is activated: when one's heart is pure, one's deeds are pure, and pure deeds make the heart even purer. Unable to forget the pleasure of doing good, one repeatedly does good whenever the occasion arises, and it becomes a habit. One who forms this habit acquires a noble character.

Christ said that he came not to be served but to serve. In the Sermon on the Mount he said, "Always treat others as you would like them to treat you" (Matt. 7:12). This is known as the Golden Rule and is a guiding principle for human harmony. Some proclaim that the golden age of humanity will arrive when the Golden Rule is always observed.

Serve others. Be kind. Help those in need. The practice of helping others is in the end the fastest means of making oneself happy.

Since helping others is in keeping with the law of nature and makes us feel good, we want to do it all the more.

The Seven Offerings That Cost Nothing

The most reported topics in Japanese newspapers and magazines these days have to do with economics. The word *economics* has a pleasant ring, since it has to do with making money. We Japanese should certainly be grateful that Japan has become a strong economic power, but it would hardly be a good thing if it meant that the only thing on people's minds were money.

One naturally wants enough money to live, and it is important to save for a rainy day. But what happens when one begins to want more and more and allows desires to run rampant? If one's entire being is overtaken by such desires, it spoils one's character and empties one of all sense of humanity. Even worse, the more one gets, the more one is attached to things, and the more avaricious one becomes. One may waste one's whole life amassing purchases, accomplishing nothing worthwhile. In short, however many possessions one acquires, in the end it is all in vain.

Left to themselves, our desires will grow and grow. The quickest way to restrain them is to share what we have. Many will say that they do not have enough to share. Such self-justification is evidence that they remain in the clutches of desire. They are exactly the kind of people for whom the giving of offerings is most important.

I have had the honor of being invited, with others, to the residence of Princess Chichibu, which is adjacent to the Akasaka Geihin-kan (the government guest house) in Tokyo, and where a large number of pheasants have taken up residence in the garden. When the princess clapped her hands, they came scurrying across the lawn and surrounded her in expectation of crusts of bread. For those of us who live in large cities, this was a most unusual sight and a remarkable gesture of hospitality. We were even more impressed when she told us that on days when she expects visitors, she feeds the pheasants slightly less in the morning, so that when she feeds them again later in the day in the presence of the visitors, they come rushing forward all the more eagerly at the sound of her clapping. This is how solicitous she is of others.

As I listened to her speak, it struck me that this is what Buddhism means by "an offering of the heart." The Buddha preached the virtue of making the "seven offerings that cost nothing"; he taught that however destitute one may be, one can always make some kind of offering. We normally think of an offering as charity, but any kind of service will do. The teaching of the seven offerings makes it clear that gifts of money or goods may be important, but are not the only things one need offer. The seven offerings are of the eye, an amiably smiling face, kind words, service, the heart, a seat, and lodging. We need not offer all of these, but everyone is capable of offering at least one or two. Let me explain some of them.

The offering of the eye means looking upon others with a compassionate eye, warmheartedly and magnanimously. One who is looked upon in this way will feel warm inside and keenly appreciated. One who gives others such joy can be said to be taking one step, then two steps, down the path toward happiness. Looking kindly on the world around us is certainly a habit we should try to cultivate.

Another offering is that of an amiably smiling face. Sometimes we scowl or look sharply at others as if to let them know we have not let down our guard. Instead, we should set aside our own feelings for a moment, and try to put other people at ease by welcoming them with a congenial expression that lets them know we are grateful for the chance to meet and talk with them. When you meet others, greet them with a smile. Such an approach will cheer whomever you meet. If everyone were capable of this sort of offering, the world would become a happier place.

The offering of kind words means speaking to others in a way that makes them happy. Some will say that they cannot endure flattery, but is that not because flattery is insincere? What really makes people happy is the feeling that they are understood. Therefore, if you speak to someone in words that are full of understanding, then you are practicing the highest form of the offering of kind words. Nonetheless, since understanding others is extremely difficult, one should at least make the effort to speak to them in a warmhearted way, with kind words.

The offering of service means helping others as much as you can. When you see an elderly person climbing a public stairway with difficulty, for instance, lend a helping hand. When a fellow worker is doing a job that must be finished soon, offer assistance. Small kindnesses and volunteer work, like tidying a local park or collecting money for social welfare facilities, are also offerings of service. Service not only gives joy immediately through the deed itself, but also spreads its merit indefinitely, by allowing those who see or hear about it to perceive the beauty of the spirit of service. Service is something everyone can do. This spirit of offering makes the world brighter, and becomes the foundation of peace.

"It is true that fish produce so many eggs to ensure the survival of the species, but it may partly be also to provide food for other kinds of fish," said the late Dr. Yasuo Suehiro, a professor emeritus of the University of Tokyo. Since fish feed other fish with many of their own eggs, is it not all the more shameful if people think only of themselves and forget to help others?

It is easy for an affluent person to offer money or goods. However, for the poor to share what they have with people who are even poorer is not so easy. Someone who does that is remarkably pure in spirit and shows a compassion approaching that of the buddhas and bodhisattvas. In O. Henry's short story "The Gift of the Magi," an impoverished young couple exchange Christmas presents. The husband sells his precious pocket watch to buy her a comb to use on her beautiful long hair in which she takes such pride. She sells her long tresses to buy him a watch chain. Thus the comb and the chain are of no use, but the author ends by saying that in their spirit of giving the couple were as wise as the Magi.

Is it not the spirit of consideration for others that brings life's finest moments? Each time one gives thought to others, a beautiful tale unfolds, and in each life a brightly colored flower comes into full bloom.

Giving is the easiest way to control selfish desires that, if given free rein, can destroy oneself as well as others.

And or Of?

It is said that a top manager's most important job is to decide on appropriate courses of action. The nineteenth-century statesman Katsu Kaishu contradicted this, however:

> People often talk of plans and aims, but of what use are they? Broadly speaking, world events cannot be foreseen. Though one may set up a net and wait for birds to fly into it, what can one do if they fly over it? Though you make a square box for me and try to put everything under the sun inside it, there are things that are round or triangular. Trying to fit these into a square box is very difficult indeed.

I myself am the sort of person who tends not to make plans. When I do, they are usually sketchy, rather directionless outlines. Especially in work like that of the World Conference on Religion and

Peace (WCRP), in which various religious leaders from all over the world cooperate, one can hardly make a plan and just push it through. It is just like trying to fit too many round, triangular, and square objects into one container. Through the activities of the WCRP, I have encountered many different kinds of people and experienced how adherents of various religions can overcome their differences to unite in one spirit.

Encounters with such people have made me realize that a certain element is common to all group members. It may arise from a natural desire for peace. Many whom I have met and worked with are not usually argumentative, easily angered, or covetous; around them spreads a bright, peaceful realm. If these people were not like this, they would not be able to contribute to world peace. Their qualities are absolutely indispensable to society.

In trying to build harmony little by little in the world around us, I believe that the single most important thing is to develop our sense of human unity.

Even spittle, while it is in the mouth, arouses no disgust. We swallow it without a qualm. Yet once we spit, in a flash it turns into something that seems unclean. When strands of our hair, which we normally take such good care of, become entangled in a brush or form a coil at the bottom of a sink, we want to avert our eyes. This is because the strands of hair no longer seem part of us. While they are part of us, we think nothing of them. In the moment they become separated, unity is lost and they become unpleasant even to look at. "Ours" has become "other."

I therefore believe that one may define love as a sense of oneness. A strong feeling of oneness is at work in a mother's affection for her child. When a baby seems to have an upset stomach, some worried mothers will even smell or lick its feces to find the cause. In their sense of oneness they feel no disgust. This sense of oneness occurs not only between parent and child, but also between lovers and married couples. When we feel it toward many people and eventually all things, we have acquired the compassion of the Buddha.

In chapter 3 of the Lotus Sutra, "A Parable," the Buddha proclaims:

> Now this triple world
> All is my domain;
> The living beings in it
> All are my sons.

Everything in the world, everything in the universe, is the Buddha's, and everything that lives is the Buddha's. These words of the Lotus Sutra express the epitome of oneness.

We must never think of ourselves and others in confrontation, but think of all others enveloped within the self as one. This may seem a truly distant goal, but by trying to approach it a step or two at a time, humanity will be lifted up.

When Yasunari Kawabata (1899–1972) received the Nobel Prize for literature in 1968, he began his acceptance speech by reading a poem by Dogen:

> In the spring, cherry blossoms, in the summer the cuckoo.
> In autumn the moon, and in winter the snow—clear and cold.

He then tried to explain the Japanese spirit and show how it has sought harmony with nature rather than confrontation.

The Zen master Mumon Yamada (1900–1988), the leader of the Myoshin-ji school of the Rinzai sect, in *Bodaishin o Okoshimasho* (Let Us Aspire to Buddhahood), said of Kawabata's speech:

> The first draft was titled *Nihon no Bi to Watakushi* (The Beauty of Japan, and I), which he altered in the final draft to *Utsukushii Nihon no Watakushi* (I of Beautiful Japan). He noted in the final draft that the title might seem presumptuous, but there was deep significance in his use in the final title of *of* rather than *and*. Kawabata also said that to speak of beautiful Japan was to speak of himself, and that unless he spoke of the Japan that nurtured him, he could not speak of himself. He and beautiful Japan were not separate, but one; hence *of* rather than *and*. *And* belongs to Western thought; *of*, in which two things are perfectly in tune, belongs to Eastern thought and the Japanese sensibility.

This explanation that *of* represents the Japanese sensibility made me completely reexamine my thinking. The Japanese have long held a conception centering on *of*. Whereas the Western home has been made of thick stones as protection against nature, the Japanese home has been *of* nature, with space between the pillars. Not sharing the Western idea that humankind has dominion over nature, the Japanese feel part of nature and try to live in harmony with it. The Japanese have never considered matter and spirit as separable. They know that things have a spirit and that true happiness and peace come from being in harmony with things and uniting with them. On this foundation, Buddhism fostered an even deeper consciousness of the idea of *of*.

The sense of oneness in the spirit of *of*, which sees the self and the other as one and the same, is, in a word, compassion. When we approach people in that spirit, the realm of happiness and peace grows. Some people may wrongly think that no ordinary person can enter that realm; but anyone who does volunteer work is already approaching it. Ordinary people think of caring for the elderly as a hardship, but the kind of person I refer to does not see it that way. The problem of care for the elderly arises only because people think of the elderly as separate, in terms of "me *and* old people." Those who willingly care for the elderly think of them as "our old people," and are glad to do it.

International disputes often go to extremes, and dissent and confrontation often end in deadlock. What will break the deadlocks and open up the future of the human race is this spirit of oneness. Jawaharlal Nehru (1889–1964), independent India's first prime minister, who had deep ties with Japan, said that the mission of Mahatma Gandhi, the greatest man of our time, was to wipe away the world's tears. Nehru said that though we may be too weak to achieve that goal, we cannot proclaim that our work is done as long as tears and anguish remain in the world.

There is no doubt that we are *of* one another. When this sense of oneness shines its bright light on the world, first in one dark corner, then gradually wider and wider, it will light up the entire world.

Seeing yourself and others as one and the same, that is, having a sense of the unity of all people—that is the Mahayana spirit and the essence of any true religion.

THE WIND BLOWING
FROM THE FUTURE

The Strong Winds of Early Spring

It is understandable that people in their fifties and sixties comment uncomprehendingly about young people's behavior and customs. But nowadays it seems that in Japan there are even people in their thirties who refer to those fresh out of college as a new breed of human beings and say they cannot understand them at all. Youth always makes its appearance on the stage bearing new ideas and goes on to create a new society. It is important to provide young people with appropriate roles and allow them to perform them according to their own abilities.

> Can you not feel
> The wind blowing from the future,
> The clear, pure wind?
> It is a ray of light sent forth—
> The determined south wind.

These lines are from the poem "To All My Students" by Kenji Miyazawa. The poem is a particular favorite of mine, and I feel that it captures accurately the distinctive qualities of youth. Some people say that Japanese young people today are spiritless and indifferent, but that is surely a transitory, abnormal phase of young people's lives, and not a cloud that will hang over them for good. As the poem tells us, youth is like a wind that blows from the direction of what is yet to come. It is therefore transparent, unclouded, and brisk. Youth celebrates a genuine, unsullied sense of justice, admires the noble and the beautiful, and is filled with vitality. Moreover, like the sun at dawn, youth is a fresh light that opens a new age.

When older people are not careful, they tend to forget that natural appreciation of the full vigor of young people. Older people too often come to consider the young as a nuisance, as immature, inexperienced people who are always apt to make a mess of things. Of course, there are also many older people who do try to understand the young, but even they sometimes seem perplexed about how to approach them and figure them out. There are also some who appear to believe that trying to understand the young means simply giving them free rein.

To truly understand young people is to grasp firmly what lies beneath their callowness, lack of refinement, and intensity, and to grasp that distinctive quality portrayed in Miyazawa's poem. Once one discerns that quality, one realizes that it is perfectly normal to have such obvious faults. In other words, one realizes that the immaturity and coarseness of youth spring from sheer exuberance. Fruit is hard and green before it ripens, yet has a juicy freshness for which it is valued. Ripe fruit may be sweet today, but is not for savoring later. That the young sometimes go too far is a perfectly natural result of their superabundant vitality.

Youthful ardor is like the strong south wind of the poem. In Japan the strong south wind of early spring revives the dormant, winter-withered fields and mountain foliage. Since it is a strong, gusty wind that suddenly arises one day when the air is still cold, for the most part people find it unpleasant. However, if one can overcome that feeling and think of the wind as one that will bring out the hard buds of the trees, then even the rattling of the windowpanes will seem a welcome harbinger.

Hence, searching out the true nature that lies beneath the surface is the way to understand youth. The older person who is neither too lenient nor disapproving is one who understands.

Albert Schweitzer said we ought not to acquaint young people with the ways of the world in such a way that we destroy their ideals, but in a way that strives to keep their ideals alive. All young people have ideals. They dislike compromise all the more because, consciously or not, they seek perfection. The real world, however, is complex and diverse, and many things cannot be clearly understood. All this perplexity frustrates

young people, and sometimes they turn to antiso-
cial behavior or a nihilist way of life. Youth carries with it this sort of danger.

The key to helping the young weather these
crises and adopt a healthy and vigorous way of
life is to entrust them with responsible tasks. I can
give virtually any young person a responsibility
and count on its successful accomplishment. Few
things are more enjoyable than watching immature, inexperienced young people come to grips
with new tasks for which they are responsible,
and grow into mature, capable people.

*It is important to entrust our fresh and vibrant young
people with appropriate responsibilities that they have
the ability to carry out on their own.*

Courage That Opens Doors

I have many hopes for young people today, and
one is that they have courage. This includes the
courage to be independent and self-reliant: the
courage to stand on their own two feet. Recently,
Japanese young people, perhaps because they
grow up in the warm, protected environment
provided by their parents and society as a whole,
seem to lack this spirit of self-reliance. I believe
that young people should be so strong that they
are afraid of absolutely nothing. They should
have the courage to accept any challenge. They
will fail sometimes, but in the process they will

develop a natural prudence. In any event, they ought to have the courage to act.

Uesugi Yozan (1751–1822), the *daimyo* (feudal baron) who restored the fortunes of the impoverished Yonezawa domain, is frequently represented as a model for business managers. Born in the household of the Akizukis, the family of a small Kyushu *daimyo*, Yozan was adopted by the esteemed Uesugi, the *daimyo* of the Yonezawa domain (in what is now Yamagata Prefecture). Yozan was seventeen at the time, about the age of today's high-school students. The Yonezawa domain, with an annual revenue of 150,000 bushels of rice, was ostensibly a large fief, but in reality it was almost insolvent. Yozan first arrived in Yonezawa on a chilly day in late autumn. As he looked out from his palanquin on village after village where even the doors of the houses were broken in, the new lord blew on the almost extinguished charcoal in his small hand-warmer. Seeing this, one of his retainers offered to bring fire immediately. The young lord restrained him, saying, "I am now learning a very important lesson. I shall tell you about it later." Arriving at his quarters, he called his vassals before him and made the following proclamation: "As I saw with my own eyes the poverty of my people, I was just about to lose all hope when I became aware that the piece of charcoal in my hand-warmer was about to go out. As I blew lightly on the charcoal it began to glow again. I wondered whether I could rekindle the same sort of flame in the heart of my domain and the hearts of my people and restore them to better conditions. The prospect fills me with hope." By thrift, the promotion of local industries, and the development of new farmlands, Yozan was ultimately successful in revitalizing his domain. That episode of the day in his youth when he saw the dismal poverty of his domain and mustered courage is well known.

That one has lost hope and fallen into despair does not mean the end of everything. It simply means that the flame in one's heart is flickering feebly. All one has to do is rekindle it.

Some people merely drift with the times and develop no backbone. When something untoward occurs, they blame society or the government. In doing this they admit their sense of absolute powerlessness in the face of their surroundings. What one needs is the strength to say, "I don't care what society is like. I'm not going to give in. No matter how bad things are, I'm going to push on through." The Meiji Restoration of 1868 was the greatest reform movement in Japanese history, and when we recall the young age of the noble patriots of those days, we feel the greatness of youth's hidden strength and courage. Takasugi Shinsaku (1839–67), a retainer of the Choshu domain, was only in his twenties when he went to Nagasaki to buy warships. The domain's confidence in him is commendable, but even more impressive is the inexperienced young man's composure in making such enormous purchases. Yoshida Shoin (1830–59) was twenty-seven when he opened the Shoka Sonjuku academy, and Sakamoto Ryoma (1835–67) was only thirty-three when he fell under the dagger of an assassin. Saigo Takamori (1827–77) lived a bit longer, but he was in his thirties when he was active in the overthrow of the shogunate. These young people devoted their entire lives to carving out a new age. True enough, feudal society was beginning to crumble, but it was undoubtedly hemmed in by walls whose thickness we in our day can hardly imagine. These youths fearlessly flung themselves against these obstacles.

Having renounced war and made the decision to adopt a pacifist foreign policy, Japan will undoubtedly face many trials in the years to come. Japan also has the potential to lead the world in a variety of ways, including the promotion of disarmament, international cooperation, and technological innovation. To bring on this new age, the vigor of youth is essential.

To meet these challenges, I hope Japanese young people will develop the courage for self-sacrifice. As we in Japan look around us today, we do not often see people who would risk their lives for their country or in the service of others. I am talking even about small acts of self-sacrifice in daily life. For example, giving one's seat in a train to an elderly person is a small act of self-sacrifice. Instead, some people remain nonchalantly seated as an older person stands nearby. When everyone makes these small sacrifices in daily life, the world goes harmoniously and smoothly.

Though the world may seem to give precedence to individual rights and self-expression, young people should not forget the spirit and pleasantness of such small acts of self-sacrifice.

Finally, the young must have the courage to challenge the unknown, to turn toward the unexplored and boldly plunge into uncharted territory. It would seem that many young people nowadays draw a blueprint for their whole life and are satisfied with merely realizing it. If that is the way it is, there is little to hope for in the way of spiritual progress for the individual, society, and humanity as a whole. Young people are brimful of energy, and I hope that they will use that energy to challenge the limits of the abilities they are endowed with. It is wrong for young people to underestimate themselves—to build a wall around their own abilities and to pace this way and that within it. If, for instance, it does seem that a wall of difficulty bars the way, by trying boldly to smash through it they can show their hidden strength and create new worlds.

Self-reliance, self-sacrifice, and a willingness to challenge the unknown—young people need these three kinds of courage.

"Even Insects Work and Eat"

My parents were farmers in a small mountain village in Niigata Prefecture. As a young man, my grandfather learned the fundamentals of medical treatment. Whenever a neighbor fell suddenly ill, Grandfather would hurry to give whatever emergency treatment he could, and he was highly thought of thereabouts. Grandfather often said that if all a family did was work and eat, they were no better than insects. After all, he said, even insects work and eat. He felt that at least one person in each family ought to be devoted to helping others. His words became engraved on my heart when I was a boy, and I believe that is why I have devoted my life to human happiness.

Just as each person has individuality, so do families. A family's character is formed by the personalities of the father and mother. Their traits have such influence on the children that what the children learn during their years at home sustains them throughout life. Compared with a hundred or even fifty years ago, our awareness of the family's significance has diminished. In old households in the provinces and elsewhere, there remain to this day maxims of great significance that have been passed down from generation to generation. There were no particular maxims in my own family, but my grandfather's favorite saying served a similar purpose. That the moral atmosphere of the family has come to be ignored nowadays is a true cause for regret.

The first director of Japan's Environment Agency, Buichi Oishi (b. 1909), aroused great controversy when he switched from the Liberal Democratic Party (LDP) to the New Liberal Club.

The circumstances of his move were complex, but it is said that as chairman of the Foundation for the Preservation of Our Green Planet, he would be in a better position to work for disarmament and environmental protection in the New Liberal Club.

Oishi's father, Rinji Oishi, had also been a politician. In 1942, the second year of the Pacific war, the military forced the government to ban all political parties except for the promilitary party. Almost everyone joined the promilitary party, except for six members of the House of Representatives who refused, one of them being Rinji Oishi. On refusing to join, Rinji wrote his son: "Even if I am the only one in the whole country to do so, I believe that sticking to my principles, hard as it must seem in Japan at this particular moment, is the only way for me to serve the country." Buichi is said to have treasured this letter ever since. Clearly, his character was strongly influenced by his father's example.

"Life is like carrying a heavy load down a long road: there is no hurry." These well-known words of Tokugawa Ieyasu (1543–1616), the warlord who established the Tokugawa shogunate, are the first of his maxims for proper conduct. Some others are

> Accept privation as normal and you will never be dissatisfied.
> When excessive desire arises, one ought to recall one's days of privation.

Endurance is the foundation of tranquillity and
   long life.
Consider anger an enemy.
When one knows only victory and no defeats,
   one is at a disadvantage.
Censure yourself, not others.

It is because these maxims were observed that the
Tokugawa peace lasted for about 270 years. Each
of these maxims remains perfectly valid today.

Another well-known set of family maxims is
that of the Homma clan of Sakata, Yamagata
Prefecture, which flourished for centuries as the
nation's largest landowner, until the agrarian re-
forms after World War II. There are twelve maxims in all, but let us look at the main ones:

Revere the gods, honor the buddhas. Do not
   neglect your devotions even for one day.
Never forget to be diligent and frugal.
Be unsparing in public-works efforts; do not be
   stingy in using assets for the public good.
The heir should travel throughout the land to
   increase his store of knowledge.
Do not seek marital ties with the wealthy;
   marry daughters from simple, stable homes.

In addition to these maxims, there was an unwrit-
ten injunction that a fourth of the family's profits
should be donated to shrines and temples, and
another fourth given in aid to tenant farmers and
the poor. The several centuries of Homma family history include the severe Temmei Famine

(1782–87), poor harvests due to damage by cold weather, and several rice riots. It can certainly be said that these family maxims played a significant role in overcoming these crises and continuing the family's prosperity.

Long ago in the homes of carpenters, the child who stepped over a toolbox got a severe scolding. Children in farming households were constantly admonished to keep the hoes and sickles carefully polished. It was the custom in merchant households, as soon as the clerks awoke in the morning, for them to sweep the street in front of the shop. If one is raised with this sort of discipline, it becomes an asset throughout life.

Even one maxim kept by a family will become a pillar sustaining the children all their adult lives.

Home Is More Than a Haven

In recent years more and more Japanese men have come to find meaning in their lives at home. At first sight, this appears to be a healthy shift in attitude. Since the family is the smallest human unit, making it happy and serene is inevitably connected with work for social harmony and world peace. The past two decades, however, have been a period of excess in Japan, in which high economic growth has been welcomed and the home has come to be considered merely a place of relaxation, family harmony, and consumption. This is hardly a wholesome view of the home.

The home is frequently likened to a port of refuge from the rough seas of everyday life. It is perfectly normal for a family to seek respite there for body and soul. However, ships enter port not only for safety but also for refitting. Repairs have to be made, and water and food taken on for the next voyage. When the home becomes almost exclusively a refuge, the atmosphere becomes too relaxed, and it ceases to be a place of self-improvement. While the home is certainly a haven, it should also be a place where family members learn together how to be better human beings.

It is certainly true that Japan's rapid modernization beginning in the nineteenth century, and its impressive resurgence since World War II, are due to the natural endowments of the Japanese people. But have Japanese mothers not forgotten that it was always the mother who was the central support and the guiding light in the home? Mothers whose children went on to become brilliant successes were without exception superior mothers.

An example is the mother of Soichiro Honda (1906–91), the founder of Honda Motor Company. Like other girls in her village, she learned to weave on completing fourth grade, and went on weaving until she was over eighty years old. Once her son became a leading industrialist, she may have gone on weaving simply as a pastime, but through the hard years of raising seven boys and two girls she weaved to supplement the family income and to provide the family with clothing.

The journalist and social commentator Saeko Saigusa quotes Honda on his mother's discipline in those days:

> I was quite a mischievous boy, so I was often scolded by my mother. Sometimes I took my pranks a little too far and I was punished and was sometimes even tied to a pillar in the house. My father and mother were truly *just* people, so they were very strict when anyone did something wrong. They did not complain to us about our school grades. Since I was the adventurous type, I sometimes got involved in things that were a little dangerous. I once entered a motorcycle race and caused an accident in which my brother and I were seriously injured. But my parents never tried to dissuade me from such activities because of the dangers.

One can tell that although he was sometimes punished physically, even as a child Honda recognized his parents' uprightness and respected them for it. That is why Saigusa writes that if there was one person that Honda, fearless daredevil though he was, could not but respect, it was his mother. In this world, having someone to respect that much is truly fortunate.

In the Chinese classics there is a saying, "A one-year plan is best for wheat; a ten-year plan is best for trees; and a hundred-year plan is best for man." This is certainly true. People thirty years old have at the very most thirty or forty more years to be active. After that they have to rely on the younger generation, the children of today.

The haven we know as the home is certainly not merely a place of rest. It is a place where one can be reinvigorated for life in the outside world, and more than anything else it is a place of education. Do parents really teach? Do they raise their children to be good human beings? Do they raise their children in such a way that regardless of their future occupations and positions, they will be of some service to the world?

Yukichi Fukuzawa wrote out some advice for raising children, which includes the following:

Children should be energetic and physically healthy.

Children should always be playing lively outside whenever they have free time, even when it is windy, rainy, cold, or hot, except in the worst weather, so that they will not become withdrawn.

For good physical health, it is not enough for children merely to frolic all day. They should also take an active part in morning and evening chores so that they will gradually accustom themselves to the importance of performing useful service.

Chores should be divided among the children of the house according to their age, and the children should carry these out themselves.

This advice is followed by a list of tasks for each child, including tidying and weeding the garden and mopping the veranda. Although there were seven or eight houseboys in the Fukuzawa household to help out, chores were carefully allotted to each child in the family.

To me, the most interesting thing is that Fukuzawa gave no advice about studying. And come to think of it, Honda says in his memoir that his parents never complained about his schoolwork. Education is a lifelong process. Its most important aim is building character, and I am entirely convinced that the foundation for this is laid in the home.

Home is a haven, not only as a place of rest, but also as a place of education where parents raise their children to be fine adults.

Where Affection and Gratitude Begin

As I look at the state of the world, it worries me considerably that the ties that bind people—parents and children, husbands and wives, teachers and students, and friends—are weakening. If the trend continues, Japanese society will lose much of its stability. It is urgent that we aim at the kind of character building that is based on a philosophy of unity rather than on one of diversity. I believe that the most important concrete method for achieving this is to strengthen the bonds that unite people and to foster a warm, tender spirit in each person.

The point of departure for all human relationships is the bond of parent and child. We all have parents or are parents ourselves. The bond between parent and child, unlike bonds in other relationships, especially that of parent and child, cannot be broken, whatever the effort. People refer to this bond as one of blood only, but the bond is life itself, and it is the mainstay of every human being. Feeling is the most powerful motivator of this bond. It is what makes human relationships both genial and beautiful. Emotion has a power that is much stronger than logic or theory.

A boy named Willie, whose parents sent him to Eton, was poor at mathematics and took a dislike to it. He wrote to his father imploring that he be allowed to give up the study of mathematics. His father replied immediately, telling him in no uncertain terms that he could not study only the subjects he liked. True study, he wrote, was tackling the subjects one was weakest in and mastering them. As Willie read this he could hardly contain his dissatisfaction, but he read on: "Willie, your father is here in this country house thinking of you always. Every single day I pray that you will grow up to be a respectable young man. I have every confidence that you will become just the kind of person this old father of yours hopes for." Those words moved the boy, and he made up his mind to do his best, throwing himself into the study of mathematics. Before long his efforts were rewarded and he obtained a perfect score on his mathematics test. He immediately sent the test paper to his father. Several days later it came back in the mail, and at the top was written, "Splendid, Willie!"

Willie was William Gladstone (1809–98), the eventual leader of Britain's Liberal Party and four times prime minister. He said often that his service to his country was due entirely to what his father had taught him as a boy. I believe that it was less what his father taught than his father's affection. Any father could have written the first half of the letter; it was the true feelings of the second half that roused the young boy.

The bond of parent and child begins at conception. From then on the child does nothing but give its parents trouble. From the sufferings of pregnancy and childbirth to the hardships and anxieties that accompany raising and educating children, parents wear themselves out for their children. Still, parents do not resent doing this. Like Gladstone's father, they constantly hope that their children will grow up to be splendid adults. That is quite natural. Moreover, it is entirely natural for children raised that way to feel affection for their parents, to be devoted to them, and to obey them. If this natural, reciprocal affection is not shown, something must be wrong.

Most people love their mothers. Perhaps some people are less attached to their fathers partly because they spend less time together. If, nevertheless, as with Gladstone and his father, they develop a strong bond, their natural affection will show.

Physical contact is also important. It is good to pat people on the shoulder when you tell them to cheer up or to tap your knuckles reprovingly on the head of a child. For Japanese fathers, getting into the bath with their children and giving their backs a good scrub is one of the best kinds of physical contact. Takeo Arishima (1878–1923), a novelist of the Shirakaba school of humanist writers, grew up in an upper-class home, and from a very young age he rarely ate with his father. He wrote that his father once challenged him to a sumo wrestling match, and that when he felt the warmth of his father's flesh as they grappled, he suddenly started to cry.

Parents treat their children as they see fit. Some parents are critical; some are lenient, letting the children make their own decisions; some strike their children when they are naughty; and some never raise a hand against their children. Since it is fundamental that parents always put their children's happiness before their own, it is a matter for each parent to decide how to treat their children. There can be no general rule.

As young people earnestly seek fulfillment and an opportunity to bloom, it is sometimes hard for them to realize how much they owe their parents. Consequently, through the schools and by other means, it is important to promote a spirit of appreciation for what parents do. Recently, in Japan, such things are not being taught at all.

Parental responsibility is stressed, and as a result, children come to feel coldly that their parents are merely carrying out that responsibility and that there is no reason to be grateful. This is a matter of grave concern, because it is connected with the forfeiture of the single most important human emotion. This kind of hardhearted way of thinking affects all other relationships, and our society becomes a desolate place where one can barely live.

The person who is truly human is one whose spirit is filled with love and gratitude. It is the person who feels affection for many and who can be grateful to many. And because affection and gratitude move back and forth within society, a world of such people becomes a truly bright, warm, congenial, human place. To create such a world, the first step must be to make the starting point, the parent-child relationship, an interaction of love and appreciation. Far from being difficult, it can be accomplished naturally by anyone willing to be flexible. Finally, we should etch upon our hearts the realization that we are all under the gentle, protective gaze of our common parent, the Buddha.

The parental bond, the starting point of human relationships, is the foundation of humanity and can never be broken by separation.

Forever Young at Heart

Almost every week I have visitors from abroad. In the belief that I should teach them something about Buddhism, I have painted three scenes: the Buddha under the bodhi tree at the moment of his supreme enlightenment; the Buddha in Deer Park, preaching his first sermon to the five ascetics who had been his fellow seekers before he gave up severe ascetic practice for the Middle Way; and Zen Master Niao-k'ê explaining to Po Chü-i the teaching of the Seven Buddhas of the Past. Tapestries based on the first and second paintings, and a ceramic plaque based on the third, are on display in the Horin-kaku Guest Hall, in the Rissho Kosei-kai headquarters complex. The first two are in the lobby, and the third is in a large private conference room on the second floor.

Although I did a little calligraphy in my youth, I had absolutely no experience with painting, and learning in middle age to paint in the traditional Japanese style was a case of "It's never too late to learn." At the age of sixty-five, I started learning from a teacher, and once I began, I found it quite interesting. I eagerly looked forward to each week's lesson, and eventually acquired the technique.

The American poet Samuel Ullmann wrote, in a poem that has become well known in translation in Japan, that youth is not only a time of life but a state of mind. People do not age merely in years, he wrote; old age comes with the loss of idealism. Few Americans have heard of Ullmann. Munehisa Sakuyama's *Seishun to Iu Na no Shi* (A Poem Named Youth) sheds light on him. A middle-aged businessman, Sakuyama spent two years in American libraries in search of even the smallest clues about Ullmann and eventually wrote a full account of his life and work.

It is important for people, as long as they live, to maintain a strong desire to better themselves and to be of service to others and to society as a whole. The secret to staying young is always to keep this desire. People like Sakuyama are good models.

The mother of Joji Tsubota (1890–1982), Japan's best writer of juvenile literature, maintained exactly that kind of youthfulness. After the early death of her husband, an alcoholic who was only occasionally employed, she worked hard to repay his debts and raise their children. By the time the children could finally make their own way, she was approaching sixty. Her sons gathered to discuss how to celebrate her sixtieth birthday. They asked her whether she would prefer a trip, a hot-spring cure, or a night at the theater. "My parents were poor," she replied, "and I wasn't allowed to go to elementary school. If you insist on my doing something, then let me go to elementary school." For a moment the brothers were dumbfounded, but because she seemed so serious, they enrolled her in fifth grade at the village elementary school. She merrily began attending. This sixty-year-old woman studied together with eleven- and twelve-year-olds and succeeded in graduating. Still not satisfied, she went on to a middle school for girls, learned to use a sewing machine and pattern-cutting equipment, and eventually became a competent dressmaker.

The average life expectancy of Japanese has risen to eighty-one years for women and seventy-five for men, the highest rates in the world. Thus it is vital that we Japanese come up with an appropriate way of viewing each time of life and devise appropriate lifestyles. If one does not attempt a major change in thinking, when one starts to grow old one will fall behind the times and spend the rest of one's life feeling lonely and miserable.

Long ago, forty-five or so was considered the start of old age. The feeling of having reached the autumn of life is rather desolate, but now things are quite different. Today, the years between the mid-forties and mid-sixties are considered the prime of life. During this period, one is deeply involved in one's work and has considerable experience, a certain well-roundedness of personality, and strength of character. If youth is the flowering of life, middle age is its abundant fruit, surely the prime of life. In terms of both work and preparation for the enjoyable later years, it is important that we live these years to the full.

There are many examples of people starting a whole new life at that age. One middle-aged person began studying for the extremely competitive bar examination and passed it at age sixty-seven. A grandmother took up the study of English and went on to qualify as an interpreter. Finally, we have the example of Ray Krok, a legendary figure in the fast-food industry, who founded his immensely successful worldwide McDonald's chain at the age of fifty-eight.

Middle age is important not only for one's work and for building one's assets, but also for laying the foundation for happy twilight years. Hobbies, study, art—any of these suffices. I heartily recommend that people take up something worthwhile that they can continue to enjoy into their eighties and nineties.

I also believe that it is important to believe in eternal life and to prepare oneself with composure for the inevitable arrival of death. Within the continuing life of the spirit, death is the turning point at which life in this world ends and new life begins. Our later years are a time for gaining a clear view of this process and calmly waiting for it. Armed with that clear understanding, we naturally feel a desire to love others, to contribute to the world, and to do good in this life. Moreover, out of this understanding, we will allow people in distress to confide in us, and we will extend a helping hand to those in pain. To choose a life of love and service is surely a fine thing.

The young tend to be very busy with their own affairs and give other people short shrift, but in later years people often become less pressed in terms of time and spirit. I believe that when we are more ready to love and help others, we can approach the transition to the next life with a contented, noble spirit.

When all is said and done, the decisive factor in attaining that frame of mind is religious faith. Those who have faith in the invisible workings of the spirit will certainly believe in the people around them. The earlier such faith is acquired, the better. If we make an early start in the right direction, we are bound to lead a good life throughout the stages of youth, middle age, and old age.

Since there is no such thing as a retirement age in private life, as long as we live we should embrace a strong desire to improve ourselves, serve others, and contribute to society.